D0474343

Engaging the Eye Generation

Engaging the Eye Generation

VISUAL LITERACY STRATEGIES FOR THE K–5 CLASSROOM

Johanna Riddle

Stenhouse Publishers
Portland, Maine

STENHOUSE PUBLISHERS
www.stenhouse.com

Copyright © 2009 by Johanna Riddle

All rights reserved. No part of this publication may be repro-
duced or transmitted in any form or by any means, electronic
or mechanical, including photocopy, or any information
storage and retrieval system, without permission from the
publisher.

Every effort has been made to contact copyright holders and
students for permission to reproduce borrowed material. We
regret any oversights that may have occurred and will be
pleased to rectify them in subsequent reprints of the work.

Due to the rapidly changing nature of the Internet, the locations of some web pages cited in the text may have changed
since publication.

Library of Congress Cataloging-in-Publication Data
Riddle, Johanna, 1958-
 Engaging the eye generation : visual literacy strategies for
the K-5 classroom / Johanna Riddle.
     p. cm.
 Includes bibliographical references.
 ISBN 978-1-57110-749-7 (alk. paper)
 1. Reading (Elementary) 2. Literacy. I. Title.
 LB1573.R53 2009
 372.4--dc22

                              2008035323

Cover design, interior design, and typesetting by Isaac Tobin

Manufactured in the United States of America on acid-free,
recycled paper

15 14 13 12 11 10 09 9 8 7 6 5 4 3 2 1

WITH DEEP AFFECTION FOR THE CHILDREN
OF SAMSULA SCHOOL, WHO ILLUMINATED
THE PATH OF LEARNING WITH JOY,
CURIOSITY, ENTHUSIASM, AND IMAGINATION.

CONTENTS

Acknowledgments

This story reflects the truth that great things can happen every day in small, ordinary, and, often, unanticipated ways. I never expected that anyone would take any special interest in the academic life of a ninety-six-year-old rural school, situated between the pasture and cornfield. Yet here I am—sharing my story with you, unfolding the whys and wherefores of the very real journey documented within the pages of this book. If nothing else, this volume serves to illustrate that we are all part of something bigger than ourselves.

My thank-you list is long. At the very top of that list sits Samsula School—the teachers, parents, grandparents, volunteers, staff members, and, of course, those wonderful waves of students who kept every single day fresh. Special acknowledgment must go to Becky Blankenship, our school media clerk, who has been a committed partner in media education; to fellow teacher Felice Freeman, whose mastery and camaraderie kept me fixed on the constant of what empowered public education can and should be; to my encouraging media mentors, among them, Dana Thompson, Irma Sue Stofsky, and Sue Ellen Shaw; and, finally, to my principal, Don Olech, who pushed me out of my comfort zone and into new arenas.

Many people enter our lives briefly, inspire and engage us, and then disappear. With that in mind, I would like to thank the high school teacher from Pennsylvania who came up to me after hearing my conference presentation on integrated literacies and said, "My principal wants me to teach this way, but I don't know how! Have you ever thought of writing a book?"

So many teachers are born with the compulsion to teach, to make whole, to bring forward. It is in the blood. In that context and as a fifth-generation American teacher, I must acknowledge James Clay Potts, John Jacob Mims, Ervie Davis Burgess, Mary Jo Burgess, James Potts, and Patricia Burgess

Potts. It is my hope that a bit of the best of you is reflected in the way that I choose to teach.

Certainly, no thank you is complete without recognizing the unceasing support of my immediate family. Unending thanks to my husband, Gregory, who picked up all of the loose ends and kept life flowing while I took on the unimaginable task of authoring an entire book. And, of course, thanks and love to my ever-supportive techno-savvy sons, James and Andrew, who filled in so many of the rough places.

One of the many wonderful effects of this project in learning was an invitation to become an Adobe Education Leader. My Adobe colleagues—among them Lisa Deakes, Deborah Hargroves, Linda Dickeson, and Sara Martin—keep me constantly connected and growing.

Certainly, thanks is due to my editor, Holly Holland, who never flagged in the belief that I had something real and rich to contribute to the learning community and who cheered me on every step of the way. Her expertise and insight proved invaluable.

And finally, I offer much love and gratitude to the Samsula, Florida, community itself. I will always be honored to have played a small role in contributing to the pride and tradition of this very special little corner of the world.

x

Introduction

You opened this book because you want to teach today's students well. You know who they are: the kids who complete their homework on one window of their computer, send instant messages through a second window, listen to a personalized playlist on their iPod, and watch television out of the corner of their eye—simultaneously. They live in a world of almost constant stimulation. Communication is frequent and multidimensional.

Today's students are often manipulators and creators of their own information and entertainment. Bombarded by visual cues, they seem to translate images and information effortlessly, communing in a conceptual world where "the thought's the thing."

You also know that it can be tough to compete with so many fascinating distractions. Standing in front of the classroom and instructing your students to open their textbooks to page forty-seven doesn't excite or motivate them. In fact, some students describe their adaptation from independent, technology-based learning to traditional education formats as "powering down" (Puttnam 2007). Educators know that students still must master traditional subjects, but the way they learn continues to evolve. So, the question is: How do we change the way we teach to best reach today's learners?

We have to link real learning to real lives. Infusing our lessons and assessments with relevance and rigor starts with good intentions, but it must be supplemented by sound practices and open minds. If we genuinely want to reach our students where they are, show them how to apply technology meaningfully and substantively, and encourage independent, critical, and creative thinking, we must be prepared to help them navigate life in the twenty-first century. This means that we can't keep looking at teaching through twentieth-century lenses. Admittedly, adapting to the challenges of this education frontier can seem overwhelming, even undoable, when confronted with scheduling, accountability, and curricular demands. There never seems to be enough time, training, or equipment to do our jobs well. We also may not know how to initiate the transformation.

I can relate to that. I reentered the classroom eight years ago, after a second career in arts administration. I had been out of touch with students on a daily basis, knew nothing about technology resources beyond email and word processing (I was a genius at pushing the *print* button), and was leaving a field in which I had been both comfortable and successful for the role of a greenhorn media educator. I was supposed to be responsible for directing the technology instruction for faculty and students. When my techno-savvy principal reeled off a list of expectations for my new job, I felt nervous and exposed. My vision of reading a witty and charming story to a circle of raptly attentive children faded. I remember wondering if I could get my old job back.

I struggled to get a grip, to master both tools and processes, to grasp the wide range of developmental levels, learning styles, and curricular needs of a campus full of students and teachers. Through this struggle, a more nuanced teaching philosophy evolved. I learned how to work smarter, to look beyond a specific discipline or grade level to applications and processes that were rich in content, meaning, and skills. I began to think about and include the wide range of literacies that comprise modern communication. As my colleague Collette Stemple so beautifully phrased it, I discovered how to balance "rigorous academics with rigorous creativity."

I also began to know my students and understand how hungry they were for meaningful engagement in learning. They wanted to *experience* education—see it, hear it, and create it. Influenced by current culture, their learning modalities were overwhelmingly visual. They wanted to "show what they know." And they all wanted to get their hands on technology. Their passion ignited my own, and our collaborative journey into the world of twenty-first-century learning sparked wonderment and illuminated the path to deeper, purposeful instruction that continues to this day.

A BROADER VIEW OF LITERACY

As our culture and communication continue to expand, the world grows ever more connected, and technology increasingly integrates our daily lives, the criteria for becoming a literate person in the twenty-first century also extends beyond traditional boundaries. Consider that the search engine Google produces more than 338,000 responses when prompted for "definition of literacy."

Although the debate persists about whether it is reasonable to address so many characteristics in our literacy framework, most educators would agree that a literate person today must be able to do more than accurately read and write text.

The North Central Regional Education Laboratory, building on the work of the International ICT Literacy Panel, identified eight essential categories of literacy in today's knowledge-based society:

- Basic Literacy: The language and mathematics skills needed to function successfully on the job
- Scientific Literacy: The ability to understand scientific concepts and processes to make good personal and social decisions
- Economic Literacy: The ability to identify and analyze the advantages and disadvantages of public policies and economic conditions
- Technological Literacy: The ability to understand and use the tools of technology to reach identified objectives
- Visual Literacy: The ability to "interpret, use, and create visual media in ways that advance thinking, decision making, communication, and learning"
- Information Literacy: The knowledge and skills necessary to find, analyze, and synthesize information using technology
- Multicultural Literacy: The ability to understand and respect differences among cultures
- Global Awareness: The ability to understand the world's interconnections (Weis 2004)

New learning standards reflect these broader views, incorporating technology, visual, and communication skills into benchmarks for traditional subject disciplines. An amalgam definition of twenty-first-century literacy might read like this:

4

reading and writing,
listening and speaking, and
analyzing and communicating

through a range of socially contextual symbols, including
texts and images,
in any combination
relevant to the individual or culture

Rather than merely "new," today's literacy is multidimensional, incorporating many different ways of receiving and expressing information and often involving creative collaboration. Visual literacy is central to such communication.

Writer John Debes coined the phrase *visual literacy* in 1969, but the idea of communicating and interpreting messages through visible actions and representations has been around much longer. Cave dwellers, drawing their images of great hunts, were documenting and archiving stories for future generations. Today's Mandarin characters are elegant refinements of ancient Chinese pictographs. Byzantine and early Renaissance artists made generous use of symbols and icons to communicate meaning to a largely nonreading public. For example, they usually dressed central figures in particular colors and included a reed or scroll to indicate that the subject was a writer, a scribe, or an educated person. Other symbols were more subtle but still suggestive, and people of the era understood the visual messages portrayed in these "art stories." When the advent of the printing press in the mid-fifteenth century made books accessible to a wider range of the population, the definition of traditional literacy—the ability to read and write at a particular level of competency—took shape and became the generally embraced mission of educators everywhere. As innovation changes the way we understand the world, our definition of literacy transforms to include new ways of interpreting information.

The Age of Information, a term signifying the shift from the primary production of physical goods to more knowledge-based industries, has included many challenges, but it also has unleashed an exciting universe of ideas, opinions, and perspectives. I first accessed the Internet in 1994 while taking a graduate course in educational media. I saw something unfolding that would revolutionize the way we learn and communicate. As an educator, I was fascinated by the richness and potential of this medium. As an art teacher and administrator, I have always been interested in the communicative aspects of visual imagery. Modern media and technology applications have refocused visual literacy. No longer an elective course of fine arts studies, visual imagery, fueled by technology and connectivity, has raced to the front and center of communication.

I also see a pressing need in education to recognize and respond to the world as our children know it. Technological innovations that once seemed exotic extravagances—the Motorola 2900 series cell phone, circa 1988, available at the hefty price of $2,000, comes to mind—now form the landscape of our everyday communications network. Today's cell phones enable 85 percent of Americans to communicate verbally, textually, and visually on a whim; to connect to the Internet; to download music, videos, or up-to-the-second stock quotes; and to take photographs, organize daily schedules, or access directions to the nearest restaurant. More than 60 percent of America's teens own their own cell phones, and more than 90 percent have regular access to one (Entner 2008).

"To succeed in the academic world, students must be proficient in both reading and writing," Mary Burns, Senior Technology Specialist at the Center for Online Professional Education (http://www2.edc.org/COPE/default .asp) in Newton, Massachusetts, reminds us. "But to navigate in the real world, they must also be visually literate—able to decode, comprehend, and analyze the elements, messages, and values communicated by image" (2006).

Such accessible tools make collaboration and information sharing a way of life. Our students were born into this world, and they explore it fearlessly. Why isn't this enthusiasm for discovery through technology a part of their daily educational landscape? It was a question that gave me, a teacher with practically zero technology skills, great pause. How could I possibly hope to empower children when I didn't even understand their world?

Blend that soul searching with a belief in the potential and power of education for all, place it within a solid framework of core disciplines, and you have an unparalleled opportunity to grow a generation of creative, multiply skilled, lifelong learners. How could a teacher possibly pass up that chance?

Developing Intelligent Vision

Everyone is looking, not many are seeing.—Peter Leschak

Educators understand that teaching a child to read text is a sequential process. We start at the beginning. We teach our youngest students the letters of the alphabet and their corresponding sounds. We help them recognize sight words and apply phonetic rules. Soon they can organize words into word families and craft simple sentences. It's a memorable moment for both teachers and students when that door of meaning swings open and twenty-six alphabetic symbols, in nearly infinite combinations, metamorphose into ideas, information, descriptions, and flights of imagination. Children's ability to make meaning from text deepens and grows as they make connections between reading and writing.

The journey toward visual literacy is much the same. It is a gradual and learned experience. Just as reading complements writing in traditional literacy, observation and creation jointly form the foundation of visual literacy. Translation is an important part of the process of developing visual literacy, as children go beyond scanning and mentally filing images to asking questions about their significance and searching for connections. As teachers, our job is to help students do more than merely look at symbols; we must show them how to interpret and communicate the meaning of images, to develop "intelligent vision."

Nature is on our side. The gleaning of information from imagery (observation) and the spontaneous urge to express ourselves through imagery (creation) are both universal to the human experience. Consider the last time you took a trip by car. You probably scanned road signs for the symbols for food, fuel, or lodging. You may have consulted road maps to help you navigate or tried to interpret the icons on creative license plates. Children similarly use images to make sense of the world.

Having listened to a story read aloud from a book, children often will "reread" the story by following the sequence and making meaning from the photos and illustrations. I observed this process closely one day when three-year-old Grayson was in the school media center with his mother. I had shared Jan Brett's *The First Dog* with a group of kindergarten students and then placed the book on a low table. While Grayson's mom perused the library shelves for chapter books for her fourth-grade daughters, Grayson settled himself on the floor and began to interpret the images in Brett's book.

READING BETWEEN THE LINES

Set in the Paleolithic era, *The First Dog* explains the domestication of wolves through the fictional characters of a young boy and a wolf that becomes his companion. Brett's richly layered illustrations help tell the story; each page contains images that explain the accompanying text but also reflect past, future, and parallel story details. With keen attention to the way a young child's mind works, Brett frames her narrative through connected context.

At age three, Grayson may not have known much about the relationship between a Paleolithic boy and a wolf, but he could draw on his knowledge of dogs and other domesticated animals to make sense of the story. Grayson's narrative was sequential. A nonreader, he interpreted the story line well. In the process of decoding the pictures aloud, Grayson used vivid descriptions such as "the mad elephant" (wooly mammoth) and "the scared boy." He announced that "now he [the boy] is hiding up in a tree."

After the next page revealed a wild-eyed saber-toothed tiger, Grayson used those images to retell, or reimagine, that part of the story, saying, "And that's [the presence of the tiger] why the boy is hiding up in the tree." Studying the final illustration, which shows the boy and wolf gazing fondly at one another while the boy fastens a leather-and-stone collar around the wolf's neck, Grayson linked the images confidently into a conclusion: "And that is when the wolf became the boy's dog!"

Figure 1.1   Kindergarten students investigate the relationship of visual and printed information in *It Looked Like Spilt Milk* by Charles Green Shaw.

Jan Brett is a brilliant "picture teller." Other authors combine language patterns with images to create meaning for young children. *It Looked Like Spilt Milk*, Charles Green Shaw's classic 1947 storybook, continues to captivate children with its simple, two-color palette; an ever-changing amorphous white shape; and patterned language. Children interpret the images by inserting their ideas into a repetitive sentence: "It looked like a ____, but it wasn't a ____!" When I read this book to my students and the illustrated white silhouette shifts from a rabbit to an ice cream cone to a pig and so forth on subsequent pages, I can almost see the light bulbs illuminated above my students' heads (see Figure 1.1). I recall the day when five-year-old Colin exclaimed, "I can't believe it . . . I'm reading!" And he was—drawing upon visual literacy skills to interpret the information and fit it together with the auditory/textual information in a way that made sense to him.

Not all imagery unfolds so clearly of course. Symbolism becomes more sophisticated and nuanced as the reading skills required to interpret text grow. For example, the cover of a junior fiction book will frequently contain more subtle messages than the cover of a preschool picture book. Yet students' visual literacy skills do not necessarily develop at the same pace as their reading levels. They need guided questioning, discussion, observation, and time to consider various forms of information before they can successfully integrate their understanding of text and images.

 For example, *Owen & Mzee: The True Story of a Remarkable Friendship* asks the question: how can two animals who are so different become friends? This nonfiction book, written by Isabella and Craig Hatkoff and Paula Kahumba, includes many large, color photographs of the baby hippo, Owen, and Mzee, a 130-year-old Alhambra tortoise, two unlikely acquaintances who nevertheless establish a bond. As I explore the issue of similarities and differences with a group of first graders, I use a Venn diagram to visually record the children's responses.

It is human nature to superficially compare and contrast, but practice is required to hone that skill into a true critical-thinking process. As a higher-thinking exercise, comparing and contrasting involves examining the characteristics of objects, people, or ideas—identifying both similarities and differences and investigating possible patterns and classifications from which we can draw general conclusions.

Explicitly teaching these skills represents another shift in our role as educators in the Information Age. We may be so focused on our students' rapid acquisition of knowledge that we neglect to teach them how to understand and apply what they see, read, and hear. At a time when access to data is instantaneous, teaching students how to interpret, evaluate, and apply information becomes more important than simply sharing new ideas with them.

In the case of Owen and Mzee, I begin by priming the children's background knowledge to set the stage for comparing the qualities of hippos and turtles.

"Hippos and turtles are both alive," one student ventures a guess.

"They both like water and grass," says another.

Our Venn diagram begins to take form (see Figures 1.2 and 1.3). We agree that both animals have four legs, and Dana points out that tortoises have their own forms of protection (the shell). She conjectures that hippos

Figure 1.2 Students share their research on tortoises and hippos through discussion and development of a whole-class Venn diagram.

Figure 1.3 Russell, Kayla, and Elana are busy developing their own Venn diagrams. They will bring their work back to share with the group and add their findings to the large classroom Venn diagram.

"probably have to hide in the water for protection." Bailey observes that both tortoises and hippos are "sort of grayish green" in color.

Next we read the story together, paying careful attention to the visual information conveyed through the photographs. As the story unfolds, students add information to the Venn diagram. They agree that

- The hippo and the turtle are both round.
- They both like the tall grass.
- They swim.
- Mzee is old, and Owen is a baby.
- They are both alone/lonely.
- They both live in Africa.
- Mzee is a turtle (reptile), and Owen is a mammal.
- They are both shy.
- They both know how to love.

I probe that last statement: "How can you tell that they know how to love? Can you show me?" I ask.

The children study the images closer.

"Well, you can see the part of the story where they become friends," says Joshua.

I ask him to show me where that transition takes place. Joshua locates photographs on opposite pages of the book. The photo on the left shows the baby hippo following Mzee. The tortoise is gazing ahead; Owen is focused on an object to his side. The photo on the right shows the animals side by side on a bed of grass, facing toward each other. Joshua points to the inner spine between the two pages. "Right about here," he says, truly reading between the pages to form a bridge of sequence between the two images.

I encourage inferential skills by asking the children to come up with that missing picture. What might have happened in between those two shots to help the animals form a bond? The first graders theorize that the animals might have stopped being afraid of each other, or perhaps they became used to each other. Maybe they had to share something and then realized "it wasn't so bad to be together." (My favorite response was from a child who conjectured that "maybe their hearts sparked.")

"One thing about hippos and turtles is that they don't smile," Christian says, "so you have to look at their bodies [body language] to see how they feel about each other."

Using Christian's theory, we revisit the images in the book in this context and make a list of visual clues suggesting the animals' companion-ability. The students make the following observations, providing evidence that they are indeed developing "intelligent vision."

After they become friends, Mzee and Owen:

- Look at or toward each other
- Touch and snuggle
- Share food and bedding
- Swim together
- Relax (nap and rest) together

"Can we take what we have learned about Mzee and Owen to create a definition of friendship that might work for both animals and people?" I ask.

Elana becomes very animated in response to this question. She jumps up and walks toward the center of our discussion circle, exclaiming, "You don't all have to be the same to be friends! You can share the things you like, and learn about interesting things you might not already know about by making all kinds of friends!"

We add, "respect and appreciate differences" and "look for things we can share" to our list of friendship indicators.

Through our guided discussion of *Owen & Mzee*, these young students have learned to "read" (decode) photographs to address the question posed by the author: How can two animals who are so different become friends? The children gathered information and formed theories based on their observations. They compared the visual information presented in the book to their prior knowledge, and then they used the text to find additional clues. The Venn diagram helped them keep track of the various perspectives until they could agree on a definition of the abstract concept of friendship. The process of using a visual organizer to record, organize, prioritize, and synthesize information has been modeled through this guided discussion.

"Now Show Me"

As early as fifteen months of age, humans learn to connect images to the objects they symbolize. For example, babies can associate a photograph of a cookie with the real dessert (Ganea, Pickard, and DeLoache 2008). As any advertising executive could tell you, two-year-olds generally can identify common products through signage, logos, and icons. At about three years of age, children develop the ability to create and communicate through imagery. Toddler "scribbles" soon evolve into symbolic images—children begin to draw circular shapes with lines extending from the shape to represent suns, spiders, and animals (see Figures 1.4 and 1.5). This so-called mandala shape (a universal symbol dating back to prehistoric times) eventually gives way to more detailed and representational art. Large circles with a few dots and dashes in the center and four lines extended to suggest limbs represent "mommy," "daddy," or "me." A curving line extending from one side identifies the drawing as the family pet, and so on.

This crash course in developmental drawing may seem more the realm of the art teacher than the generalist or media specialist, but the Age of Information and the technology that goes along with it has landed visual literacy in the lap of every teacher. George Lucas, filmmaker and founder of the George Lucas Educational Foundation, has definite views on the immediacy and importance of including visual literacy education in all classrooms: "When people talk to me about the digital divide, I think of it not being so much about who has access to what technology as who knows how to create and express themselves in this new language of the screen. If students aren't taught the language of sounds and images, shouldn't they be considered as illiterate as if they left college without being able to read or write?" (Daly 2004).

Media images saturate our students' lives, yet children often sit passively in front of televisions, movies, and computers, receiving and absorbing the "language" of the screens without developing critical awareness of what they are seeing. They are bombarded with print images whose purpose is to entertain or persuade young audiences that the product is desirable, perhaps essential. Conversation, analytical thinking, and simple kines-thetic activities can transform visual stimulation into true visual literacy by empowering children to communicate in the "language of images."

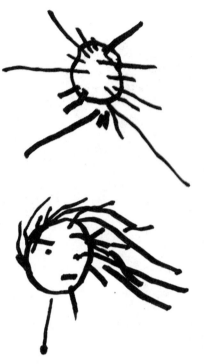

Figure 1.4 As young children develop, their scribbles transform into mandala shapes. Connecting their drawings to real objects is another step for young learners. The two-year-old who drew this mandala identified his drawing as a spider.

Figure 1.5 This three-year-old created a more detailed mandala, adding lines to represent legs and a few dots and lines to represent facial features. He identified this simple human form as "mommy with hair all around."

Just as reading and writing work hand in hand, visual interpretation and creation have a special symbiosis. Children need to apply the same analytical processes to the creation of their own imagery as they do to the analysis of visual information. How do we help them become more conscious of the critical choices that they make when they form an image?

Let's return to our group of first graders who previously interpreted photographs of Owen and Mzee and connected that visual information with the story line. Now I invite the students to "show me" what they understand about friendship through a collage image. The activity is part of a three- or four-day multidisciplinary literacy unit that addresses state-mandated studies on animal habitats and biodiversity. Creative scheduling and conversations with the classroom teacher help me blend science, geography, and language arts concepts. The unit includes small-group learning centers, one of which incorporates digital photography to help the students learn and apply technology skills.

Owen & Mzee is one of a series of books that I selected to chronicle unlikely friendships. Other fiction and nonfiction stories pair a polar bear

Figure 1.6 Diamond and Haley make some decisions about the selection and placement of objects for their "friendship" collage.

and a North American brown bear (*Little Polar Bear Finds a Friend* by Hans DeBeer); a baby bat and three baby birds (*Stellaluna* by Janell Cannon); and a gorilla, a human, and a kitten (*Koko's Kitten* by Francine Patterson). Using construction paper and markers, I created simple, two-dimensional representations of these characters. (I could have elected to scan and cut out images from the stories themselves.) I also made several cutouts of children, drawn paper-doll style, with a variety of hairstyles and skin tones, and some clothing choices. In addition, I provided a box of three-dimensional items—ribbons, silk leaves, rocks, shells, and other texturally interesting objects (some of which relate to prior lessons, such as those focusing on leaf shapes and the seasons of the year). I retrieved some shallow cardboard boxes (the kind that hold canned soft drinks) from the teacher's lounge and lined them with scraps of burlap. The boxes are proportionately perfect for framing photographs and will serve as a valuable guideline for the children as they learn to position horizontal images inside the viewfinder of their digital cameras.

Working in pairs, the first graders select, arrange, and organize materials to form their images of friendship (see Figure 1.6). They combine the physical work of creating a collage with the mental process of communicating friendship and drawing on prior knowledge of relationships. As they work collaboratively, they engage in conversation that helps them explain and critically evaluate their choices.

"Can a polar bear and a person be friends?" asks Alicia, as she selects two images to place in the cardboard tray.

"I think it's okay," says her partner, Kayla. "People take care of polar bears in the zoo."

"Well, let's put a helmet on the boy, just in case," suggests the always-practical Alicia. "And let's use that boy [selecting a figure with blond hair] because he looks like my friend, Aydin."

Next, the students take turns using a digital camera (a sturdy, inexpensive model with a wrist attachment) to photograph their collages. I had previously demonstrated how to frame a shot and press the shutter release. As the students finish, I download their images onto a computer.

From Story to Imagery—and Back Again

While some students complete their collages, others sharpen their visual skills at the computer center. Another group matches pictures and words, linking visual and textual information, at the Word Wall center.

At the science table, children have been examining a range of natural materials, working together to categorize them in various ways, including shape and texture and the object's relationship to its natural environment, such as a piece of sea coral to an image of a reef or a pressed leaf to a forest scene. Russell, holding up a whelk shell, turns it horizontally and says, "Now it looks like a triangle, but if you look at it this way [he peers at it head on] it looks like a circle." This observation lays a great foundation for talking about the concept of a writer's viewpoint.

Several students have gathered to assemble a large geography floor puzzle. They identify continents then match images of animals and simple vocabulary words—*hot, dry, forest,* and so on—to regions of the world. Some enterprising students figure out that they can combine image and word cards to create rebus sentences: "(image of penguin) lives in cold, icy (image of Antarctica)."

Other first graders have been busy at the book center, enjoying both electronic books and traditionally formatted publications. All of these activities require the interplay and interpretation of visual, textual, and auditory skills.

After everyone has had an opportunity to create a collage, I use computer software to link the visuals together in a slide show (see Can You See It? Slide Shows for more information).

CAN YOU SEE IT? SLIDE SHOWS

Slide shows create a sequence of still images. Remember the old slide show carousel in the back of the classroom? This is an updated version.

Computer software enables students to combine text and images and add audio narratives. We use Adobe Photoshop Elements and Microsoft PowerPoint. Both programs provide online tutorials for students and teachers. Adobe Photoshop Elements (http://www.adobe.com/ap/products/photoshopelwin/?promoid=BPDEM) has two, easy-to-use audio tracks, which let students integrate audio narrative, music, and sound effects. Microsoft PowerPoint (http://www.microsoft.com/education/tutorials.mspx) provides ready-made layouts that easily guide students through the process of combining imagery and text. Using the programs, students develop creative transitions between slides and add special effects that animate or emphasize selective elements in the slides.

We often link slides into presentations that either provide context or synthesize learning. For example, each student might contribute a different facet of research in preparation for a whole-group literature study and combine their visual and print findings in slide form. The group presentation provides an overview of background information that helps us better understand the story.

As a summative assessment of learning, students might contribute to a culminating project that provides a picture of their research and understanding of the topic. As they become more comfortable and competent with the process of creating and linking slides, students use slide-show formats to develop their own digital stories. They also might collaborate with a partner or a small group to develop related images and text, adding their own narration, music, and special effects.

We meet once again as a group to discuss and analyze the photos and add a text interpretation to each image. I post the student-generated indicators-of-friendship list next to a Mylar screen, and as we look at the images with an LCD projector, the list serves as a guideline for evaluating each image in terms of its effectiveness in visually communicating friendship.

"I like the way that the animals are close together," one student observes as the first image emerges on the screen. We talk about the different ways that the choice of images conveys a person's perspective about friendship.

"We added the flowers to show that their friendship is fresh and pretty,

Figure 1.7   In this example of visual messaging, a first-grade student chooses a magnifying glass to symbolize looking and arranges red tinsel to symbolize "happy thinking about." The flower and the red balloon are both positive images and also correlate to the idea of being happy. The choice of clothing for the paper figure indicates soccer.

and the sparkly tinsel shows they are having fun together," one student explains about another image (see Figure 1.7).

We work as a class to develop descriptive sentences for each image within the context of friendship and add the textual information to the bottom of each frame. Finally, we use the slide sorter to edit and rearrange our work. With the addition of a title page, author credits, and text, our collection of collages coalesces into a digital storybook. More importantly, it serves as a demonstration of developmentally appropriate mastery of visual literacy. The students have shown me that they understand and can communicate an abstract concept through imagery. In addition, they applied the technology skills required for digital photography. And they have engaged in collaborative problem solving and critical evaluation of student outcomes. The process of creating a visual story together will come in handy as students continue to expand their technology skills, learning how to create their own slides and digital stories.

SHARED STANDARDS

As we see the learning process unfold in the friendship project, we gain a greater appreciation of how smoothly visual literacy and traditional literacy can align. Let's take a look at the relationship between these two forms of information sharing and the way they contributed to the learning of a first-grade class.

LANGUAGE ARTS STANDARDS REQUIRE that students predict what a passage is about.
VISUAL LITERACY CONTRIBUTES TO THIS by guiding children through critical interpretation of accompanying images.
WE SAW THESE LITERACIES WORKING TOGETHER when students interpreted the images to predict when Owen and Mzee became friends.

LANGUAGE ARTS STANDARDS REQUIRE that students increase comprehension by re-reading, retelling, and discussion.

VISUAL LITERACY CONTRIBUTES TO THIS by providing opportunities for students to create visual interpretations of concrete and abstract concepts within a story.

WE SAW THESE LITERACIES WORKING TOGETHER when students developed collage representations of the abstract concept of friendship.

LANGUAGE ARTS STANDARDS REQUIRE that students determine the main message or idea and identify supporting information.

VISUAL LITERACY CONTRIBUTES TO THIS by organizing, prioritizing, and presenting information graphically.

WE SAW THESE LITERACIES WORKING TOGETHER when students developed a Venn diagram comparing and contrasting the characteristics of hippos and tortoises.

LANGUAGE ARTS STANDARDS REQUIRE that students make a plan for writing that includes a central idea and related ideas.

VISUAL LITERACY CONTRIBUTES TO THIS by teaching children to make thoughtful selections and interpretations of imagery within the context of a particular concept or idea.

WE SAW THESE LITERACIES WORKING TOGETHER when students developed a list of indicators that Owen and Mzee are friends.

LANGUAGE ARTS STANDARDS REQUIRE that students carry on conversations with another person, seeking answers and further explanations of the other's ideas through questioning and answering.

VISUAL LITERACY CONTRIBUTES TO THIS through collaboration and creative problem solving in the development of meaningful imagery.

WE SAW THESE LITERACIES WORKING TOGETHER when students paired up to develop collage images that expressed the concept of friendship.

LANGUAGE ARTS STANDARDS REQUIRE that students understand that their word choices can shape ideas, feelings, and actions.

VISUAL LITERACY CONTRIBUTES TO THIS through the thoughtful inclusion and arrangement of imagery, color, and text with the intent to communicate.

WE SAW THESE LITERACIES WORKING TOGETHER when students created visual interpretations of the concept of friendship, then developed descriptive sentences to accompany the photographs they produced.

Using simple materials—a book, chart paper, a few cardboard boxes, some collage materials, a digital camera—and some planning and management, a convergent learning experience unfolded. The friendship project required higher-thinking skills, encouraged collaboration, and involved students creatively and kinesthetically. It guided them through expression and evaluation of an idea in visual, textual, and linguistic formats. When students are engaged in multimodal, multiliteracy projects, you can count on a whole lot of learning going on.

FURTHER IDEAS FOR LAYERING VISUAL LITERACY

Here are a few more strategies for honing and integrating visual literacy skills. In the spirit of convergent learning ("working smarter, not harder") these activities fuse literature, technology, and creative and critical thinking skills. Whole-group sessions allow discussion and demonstration of new concepts. We also work as a whole group to evaluate our outcomes. Small-group activities provide time for learners to work at their own pace, to consider a problem from different perspectives, and to make the best use of limited resources such as digital cameras and computers. None of the projects are too high tech—the technology applications are as simple as scanning an image or clicking a digital camera—but they teach basic technology and visual literacy skills that students can build on in future years.

   Because I introduce these as primary-grade projects, they also include concrete tasks, such as manipulating tools or physically sorting and arranging objects. However, the same concepts can be adapted to encourage the development of more abstract thinking in the intermediate grades, substi-

Figure 1.8 Sierra freely combines imagery and text to form a list of objects included in Edward Lear's *The Owl and the Pussycat*. Interestingly, her list includes objects mentioned in the print narrative and objects depicted in the illustrations.

tuting software and photo-editing tools for actual objects. (There are many examples of this technology at work in subsequent chapters.)

The lessons follow the same framework as the friendship project: introducing a work of literature, discussing and analyzing the information, applying a technology process, synthesizing visual and traditional literacy to solve a problem, and evaluating outcomes. They all move from whole group to small group and back to whole group.

Visual Book Reports

Students in the elementary grades can't get enough of the I Spy picture riddle book series by Jean Marzollo and Walter Wick. These highly visual books feature collage photos—either set up as a scene or piled in a clutter. Captions below each photo are phrased in the form of rhyming riddles and ask the viewer to search for and identify specific items within the imagery. We use the I Spy concept to develop visual book reports. After selecting a book from the school media center, students generate a list of objects mentioned in their particular story. Though most students will generate a written list, some will incorporate images as well (see Figure 1.8).

We staple the completed lists to paper lunch bags and send them home with a note to parents requesting that they help the student collect representations of the objects. Back in the classroom, as they evaluate and discuss their gathered items, some children discover that they need to amend, expand, or edit their lists. For instance, after rereading *Baby Alligator* (Clarke 2000), Brandon realized that the five plastic alligators he brought to represent the book did not tell the whole story. So he added an egg, a toy fish, some grass, and a plastic bag of water to his list.

During our next lesson, I demonstrate the procedure for scanning to create a digital image of the collected objects. The scanning station becomes a small-group learning center as students arrange their objects on a tray, cover the arrangements with opaque fabric, and scan the creations to visually represent their stories.

After completing this interpretation, the children move to the writing center to add text to the imagery. Using words from their lists, they create a series of simple questions and sentences. For example:

- Do you see a net?
- Can you find a ball?
- I spy a rope.
- Can you see it, too?

Using a slide program, I format the imagery and text side by side (see Figure 1.9).

In a third learning center, students put their digital photography skills to work. Working in pairs, they create portraits of each other holding selected library books. When we meet again in a whole-group session, we use the slide sorter in a computer software program to match the portraits with the I Spy photograph and sentences.

I see a bee. Do you see a leaf? I see a flower. Do you see the apple? I see a bear. Do you see the honey nest? I see a honey pot. Do you see the worm?

The Big Honey Hunt by Stanley and Janice Berenstain

by Jillian

Figure 1.9 Imagery and text work side by side to identify the main and supporting elements of Jillian's visual book report about *The Big Honey Hunt*.

Figure 1.10 Dorsey's digital story, "I Spy an Interesting Place." The accompanying audio-track says, "I spy shells shaped like bells/a crab hotel/did someone yell?" His classmate, Ashlyn, worked with Dorsey as a behind-the-scenes producer, collaborating on concepts, storyboards, and photographs. Dorsey did his own editing and final cut.

After we have a group discussion about reading for detail and expressing the main ideas of a story visually, students use the computers to print bookplate-sized copies of the photos and accompanying text to attach to the inside cover of the corresponding children's book. This serves to motivate future readers to look more carefully for details.

Older students will sometimes revisit these early learning initiatives, applying new skills to develop more sophisticated interpretations of an idea. For example, Dorsey learned how to visually represent the main idea and supporting details from a text when he was in first grade. Later, as a third grader, he developed a series of rich photo collages and paired them with sophisticated rhyming clues in a digital story format (see Figure 1.10). His inspiration won an award at the International Student Media Festival.

Understanding Context: Picture Riddles

Students' interest in particular books, imagery, or topics often sparks unanticipated learning experiences. Such was the case when Austin, a first grader, checked out a copy of *Look Again* by Tana Hoban. Hoban has crafted a range of image-based books that encourage young children to examine the world around them. *Look Again* became a springboard for a photography project that helped students understand context. This particular book is formatted with a series of black-and-white photographs, each one preceded by a die-cut, square page that reveals a segment of the image. When readers encounter the cropped photos, they must observe the images and use visual clues and prior knowledge to figure out what the object might be before they turn the page and discover the subject in full detail. For example, a series of concentric arches in a close-up frame turns out to be a photograph of a tire and hubcap.

Austin was having a great time showing a cropped portion of a black-and-white photo to a captivated audience of his friends, encouraging them to guess what the image was. After a few minutes of his animated guessing game, he looked up and said, "I think I could make pictures like that."

Indeed he could, and a new grade-wide learning project was born.

For intermediate students, *National Geographic Kids'* "What in the World?" provides an excellent and age-appropriate springboard for a similar creative application of visual problem solving. A regular feature of the

Figure 1.11 After studying Tana Hoban's *Look Again*, first-grade students manually crop photographs to give them a hands-on understanding of the digital process.

magazine, this mystery photo game features macro photographs of common objects and challenges readers to identify items based on the isolated and magnified imagery provided. Sharpening their digital photo skills, students set out in small groups to shoot pictures around the school campus. They chose their subjects with a simple problem to solve: How can I best create a picture riddle? Finding a solution for this drove their subject and angle choices. For example, a bird's-eye view of a water drain or a vertically angled shot of shoe tread provided a more compelling visual challenge than did a child's face or a flower. The process required analysis, creativity, and visualization. The photos had to be complex enough to form a picture puzzle when cropped but become easily recognizable when the entire photo was revealed.

After I printed proofed copies of their photos, the first graders used a cropping frame to manually isolate an area of their photo (see Figure 1.11). I demonstrated the way that technology could be used to crop photos (see Can You See It? Electronic Cropping Tools for more information) and organized the finished work into a PowerPoint slide show to create an electronic book.

CAN YOU SEE IT? ELECTRONIC CROPPING TOOLS

At one time or another we've probably all taken photographs so wide that they obscured the focus. Cropping photos helps us get to the point of the picture by zooming in on a selected image. Just about every digital photo program includes a cropping tool. Picasa is a free digital photo software program, and it comes with tutorials (http://picasa.google.com/support).

We use Adobe Photoshop Elements in our classroom. You can find a step-by-step tutorial about cropping photos with Adobe Photoshop Elements at http://graphicssoft.about.com/od/digitalphotography/l/blps_prep.htm. Students select the cropping feature from the toolbar on the screen and drag it across the image they want to keep. Cropping tools make it easy to reshape photos, too. We resized our photographs from rectangles into squares for this project.

Once you click the computer mouse, the cropped photo will appear on the screen. You will want to give your photo a new name so you can save both the original and the cropped versions of your picture. I like my youngest photographers to manually crop their photographs so that they will understand what is happening when they evolve to the more abstract process of digital editing.

Students enjoyed a creative brainstorming session during our next media lesson, as they tried to guess what the cropped portion of the photos might suggest. I took the idea a step further by creating statements that included unfamiliar words. For example, I combined the statement, "I ate a xigua" (Chinese watermelon) with a demonstration of three objects: a baseball, a toy car, and a small watermelon. The first graders used the context of the words they understood—I ate—to deduce the meaning of xigua. Linking visual information to reading comprehension, we talked about the way that we could use this skill in our reading then practiced with the books they had selected from the library.

The activities described in this chapter create a solid foundation for visual literacy throughout the elementary grades. Literature and problem-based learning play a central role in these processes, and technology applications often provide the mortar to hold it together. Like the traditional reading teacher, I am building skill on skill, concept on concept to help students gain proficiency as readers and creators of many formats of information. Could we use these beginning strategies with intermediate students? Absolutely! The observations, graphs, and theories will be more sophisticated, but disaggregating the visual data leads to the same synthesis, visual awareness, and creative problem solving. Once we unlock the door to intelligent vision, we set the stage for richer understanding and communication. We begin to grow and encourage what journalist Linda Ellerbee calls "savvy interpreters of meaning."

Learning by Leaps and Layers

I'm very happy when I finish a [visual] project. It's a lot of fun getting all through it and learning new things about it. It makes me feel great! Because I can actually look at it and say "I did this . . . and I didn't need any help!"—April, age 10

In the weeks before starting my new job as a school media specialist, I did what I could to transform the ninety-year-old library into an attractive and inspiring learning environment for my students. The wood-framed windows, high-barreled ceilings, and suspiciously slanting floors (several months later, the oddly sloping north side of the 1926 floor would give way completely, resulting in the total evacuation of the media center while the foundation was rebuilt) served as a picturesque background. I added a colorful area rug, updated the bulletin boards and signage, and attached framed art to the walls. I brought in some smaller chairs and stuffed animals to make the reading centers and independent learning areas more child friendly. I cleaned out drawers and cabinets and drew up a plan of attack for transforming the stage area, which housed decades of damaged books and obsolete equipment, into the world's smallest closed-circuit television studio. Embarking on some tentative weeding of the collection, I discovered a 1926 edition of *Bambi* by Felix Salten and a science book that opened with the phrase, "If you could see the earth from space . . ." Clearly, we had a long way to go before we could comfortably call our educational resources relevant. I ordered a set of Florida's Sunshine State books (part of a statewide motivational reading program for students in grades three through eight) from my whopping annual budget of $968.

In addition to updating the physical surroundings, I tried to jump-start my thinking. I read *Information Power* (American Association of School

Librarians and the Association for Educational Communications and Technology 1998) cover to cover, studied our language arts standards, and cruised the Internet for elementary-level lesson plans, many of which I printed, placed in plastic sleeves, and organized in a four-inch notebook. Some of the empowered and committed media specialists in our school district made time to talk with me and offer advice while I took copious notes. Clearly, I was a teacher obsessed.

I admit that I wasn't completely clear on the scope of my role or of my mastery of the details therein, but I took comfort and courage in the fact that I had control of my environment, familiarity with the curriculum, and an understanding of my new area of specialization. I proactively sought to assume the traits I wished to acquire—a rather erudite way of saying, "Fake it till you make it." I needed to feel prepared for the challenges that lay ahead. I was completely certain of only one thing: I was going to grow, or die trying.

Enthusiastic and hopeful, I arrived about forty-five minutes before the first bell, of the first day, of the first school year of this millennium. The school principal greeted me and casually asked me to take digital photos of the students arriving, putting particular focus on our new kindergarten students. So I grabbed the one Mavica camera in our school inventory, inserted a floppy disk (remember those?), and traipsed to the student drop-off area, all the while muttering, "I think I can, I think I can." At that precise moment, I received my very first lesson in Technology 101: "In order for most peripheral devices to function, they must be fully charged. This process requires that they be plugged into a working electrical outlet for a suitable length of time."

That grounding aha! was the beginning of a long, upward climb toward technology literacy and application. Once I located the instruction manual, played around with the camera for a bit, and overcame the notion that "if I didn't know all about it, I wouldn't use it at all"—fear can be a powerful deterrent—I began to see the possibilities of integrating photography into the learning process. That old Mavica became a great teaching tool, the terra firma of the way that my students and I would eventually teach, learn, and communicate.

LEAP, AND THE NET WILL APPEAR

It didn't take long to realize that every child in the school wanted to get their hands on that digital camera. They saw me clicking around campus, honing basic digital photography skills, and they wanted to try it too. They wanted to experience education, not just read about it or listen to a teacher talk about it. Their hunger for a broader forum of communication and creation encouraged me to overcome my first hurdle in this new world of technology application. That moment of cognizance remains one of the great epiphanies of my teaching career—realizing that my students' need to know superseded my need to know it all. I finally understood that I didn't have to have full mastery in order to empower them. I simply had to be willing to learn alongside them, to trust in my judgment and experience along the shared path of learning. That insight changed so much about the way I had always viewed my role as a teacher. It was a definition that shifted and broadened as I realized that we were all going to move forward—together.

When I asked my students who knew how to use a computer, every hand in the classroom shot up because they all knew how to play a video game. But what computer software marketers often term *interactive* is in truth often quite passive, at least cerebrally. The fingers might be moving, but the mind remains at rest. I had something else in mind. My task would be to transform my keyboard-stroking students into empowered communicators and creative problem-solvers, to help them begin to see the computer, software, and peripherals as tools that they could control and manipulate, and not the other way around. And I was determined to do that—just as soon as I figured out how to do it myself.

I had my own radically upward learning curve to navigate. I had an inkling of the relevance of visual literacy and technology within the greater framework of K–5 but was just beginning to grasp how truly central they were to the world of today's students. Although I had a strong background in visual arts education, I was technologically illiterate. I didn't understand computers. In fact, they intimidated me. Before I could integrate those tools meaningfully, I needed to educate myself. There were avenues of learning at my disposal: district-sponsored workshops, online tutorials, independent study, conference workshops and presentations, and eleventh-hour advice from my techno-savvy teenage son (whose cell phone number I kept on speed dial), along with many, many hours devoted to playful learning. Before long, I felt armed and supported enough to take that initial leap.

I drew on a curriculum I developed several years earlier for a museum-sponsored photography camp for children. Through demonstrations and small-group hands-on sessions, the children learned about framing, points of view, and light sources—considerations for successful photographs in both traditional and digital formats. Because we were still in the age of the floppy disk, we transposed the images to the computer by inserting the disk. That part was easy enough. But manipulating and integrating the images required an understanding of the various drives, programs, and files within a computer, as well as how to bring them together. This was a confusing concept, until I hit upon a concrete illustration of these abstract maneuvers.

A jewelry box, with a series of small drawers, was pressed into service as a visual teaching tool for my students. Fixing an image of a desktop computer on the back of the box, I labeled each of the drawers on the front face accordingly: Desktop, Peripheral, A Drive, C Drive, D Drive, H Drive (our networked drive). I printed out a series of miniature photos and documents and placed them in the various drawers of the jewelry box. Using the drawers as an analogy for computer drives, I was able to show students how files could be moved from one drive to another, how files must be in the same drive to be integrated, and so forth. It wasn't high tech, but it was effective. One of my former students, now in high school, recently told me, "Whenever I sit down at the computer, I still see those drawers."

The Motivation and Inspiration of Digital Imagery

Our first activities focused on integrating the software we had on hand—Microsoft Photo Editor, Corel Paint, PowerPoint, and Word—all in tangent with our lone Mavica camera. We began simply, with a straight shot and some text overlay. Our aim was finding answers to a basic question: What is a *good* photo? We also wanted to learn how to use manual and digital tools that would help us research and answer that question. In the process, we plunged into a study of the communicative nature of imagery, exploring the symbiosis of symbols and text.

References to Henry David Thoreau in *My Side of the Mountain* by Jean Craighead George prompted a research project by a fourth-grade literature circle. Students used text and online sources to glean information that would help them compose a philosophical statement based on Thoreau's ideas and experiences. Our Florida Sunlink interlibrary loan service (http://www.sunlink.ucf.edu) came in handy, as we had few grade-appropriate texts in our own collection. Because our rural campus is bordered on all sides by forest, field, and pasture, the students were able to shoot a series of nature-inspired photos right on the school grounds. I divided the students into groups of three or four and gave each child a floppy disk, then sent them out with a partner to photograph while others in the group were busy with research and writing.

The relationship between imagery and text (see Can You See It? Combining Imagery and Text for more information) came into sharper focus as the students critically examined their photos and selected a single shot that would best reflect the statement they had created. They used a photo-editing tool to crop their photos—for subject emphasis, to enable the best placement of their text overlay, and to meet the horizontal layout of PowerPoint slide format.

CAN YOU SEE IT? COMBINING IMAGERY AND TEXT

Words and pictures go together like "peas and carrots"; each enhances the other to create a fuller range of meaning. My students use a combination of images and text in their work, often in creative formats such as poetry, subtle messaging, and graphic design.

To add a text overlay to a Microsoft PowerPoint slide, you must save the photo as a background. Then you will be able to add a text box on top. This method works best with horizontal images because the program resizes the photo to fit the dimensions of the slide. PowerPoint has Word-Art options too. These colorful, preselected font styles are popular with students and can be easily placed and resized. (You can see how Dorsey used WordArt in his photo collage in Figure 1.10 in the previous chapter).

Later we discovered Adobe Photoshop Elements and began to use this program to combine words and pictures. Photoshop Elements creates pictures in layers. A photograph can be used as the first layer of a project, and then the text tool used to form the second layer. The second layer is transparent, with the exception of the text, so the bottom layer shows through. Photoshop Elements offers a nearly limitless array of fonts, sizes, and colors. As students become more comfortable with Photoshop tools, they can add shadows, bevels, and other fancy elements to create more sophisticated presentations.

The visual literacy connections clicked immediately for some students. An upshot of a large pine tree, which Vicki captured digitally, provided a visual link to her original interpretation of Thoreau's philosophy: "Take care of nature, and nature will take care of you" (see Figure 2.1).

The photo assignment challenged Josh who was working with Thoreau's abstract advice to "go confidently in the direction of your dreams." Josh solved the problem beautifully by finding a bird's-eye view of grass growing through a pool of water. The visual effect was a stunning collage of abstract elements, including shadows, sparkling water, and reflections (see Figure 2.2). Later on, we would learn how to apply photo filters to create these types of artistic and abstract images.

The fourth graders extended their understanding of text and imagery connectivity as they experimented with the font style, size, and color for their messages. Elementary school students tend to favor certain font styles (Jokerman and Chiller are always popular choices with the under-twelve graphic designer), but simple activities help them identify properties inherent in font design. For example, the style, width, weight, size, and color of particular font designs suggest certain characteristics, emotions, and attitudes. Helping students make the connection between idea and image adds subtle impact to their visual communications. In one exercise, students selected five or more words from a list that included *happy, mean, brave, young, historic, angry, asleep, fun, bully,* and so on. They created a word picture, in which each idea is emphasized by thoughtful selection of font, size, and color (see Figure 2.3).

Figure 2.1   Vicki's interpretative image and statement, inspired by her research on the philosophies of Thoreau.

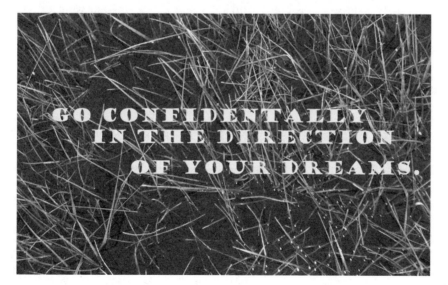

Figure 2.2   Josh used cropping tools to develop a beautiful abstract shot.

Figure 2.3 Students begin to discover the communicative value of font styles, sizes, and colors.

Within this simple project on Thoreau's philosphies, students were able to visualize and interpret the relationships among key elements of expression and use text, imagery, and fonts to effectively communicate an idea. At the same time they broadened their computer skills, successfully integrating two software programs and a peripheral device. They were able to access various drives to store and retrieve the files they needed. Skills, processes, and inquiry synthesized into a demonstration of understanding of Thoreau's philosophies and sensibilities. It was a good start. These fourth graders added to their growing toolbox the following school year, this time as project leaders, when their teacher initiated a digital poetry project that involved all fifth-grade students. (By this point, we had added two more digital cameras to our inventory, purchased with PTA funds). With "pay-it-forward" peer mentoring, the students showed classmates who had not participated in the Thoreau project how to integrate original imagery and original poetry, linking their creations through an electronic anthology of student work.

Words and Pictures

C. Denise Johnson, a professor of developmental reading at William and Mary College, reminds us that "the magic of children's literature is necessarily bound up with the nature of their development" (2003). She encourages teachers to view books through that lens of child development. As we do, we begin to see how language acquisition, reading skills, and literary devices build on one another to add sophistry and nuance to the tools of traditional literacy.

Those very first picture books were meant to be read aloud to a child, to link simple language with rich visual information. The textual content is small, the ideas concrete. Wordplay—alliteration, repetition, and rhyme— is usually integral to the communication of meaning. The language patterns within these stories contribute to the amazing rate of vocabulary acquisition among toddlers and prereaders who add an average of nine new words daily to their oral language tree. By the time these children enter kindergarten, they will have amassed a vocabulary of approximately 14,000 words. Four- and five-year-olds understand metaphor and sometimes use it as a device to fill in missing vocabulary, or to emphasize an idea. One of my favorite examples of this was five-year-old Natasha who asked to go see the school nurse, colorfully explaining her headache by saying, "My head, it is a burning volcano."

First-reader books for five- and six-year-olds focus on word recognition, vocabulary acquisition, and sentence structure. By the ages of seven and eight, most students will have gained functional fluency, able to independently read simple chapter books such as Cynthia Rylant's Henry and Mudge series or Marjorie Sharmat's Nate the Great books. At this stage, students' vocabulary has broadened and their understanding of language has deepened. They can grasp humor in multiple word meanings, such as those in the Amelia Bedelia series by Peggy Parish. They love the language of riddles and jokes. And they are able to appreciate plot and quirky characters.

Many teachers begin emphasizing literature over language as they introduce books to intermediate readers. Children ages nine to twelve are able to look deeper within a story line, to begin appreciating such literary subtleties as subplots, symbolism, themes, and character motivation. (One colleague, observing a fifth-grade literature circle discuss *Touching Spirit Bear* by Ben Mikaelsen said, "These kids discuss books like they discuss movies!") Their language acquisition, though slowed considerably, will still exceed 30,000 words by the time they become young adults.

Naturally, children's literature increases in sophistication and depth as they grow. Language arts benchmarks and standards reflect this. Kindergarten-through-grade-two reading benchmarks aim to predict passages, identify words, construct meaning, increase vocabulary, and improve comprehension. Benchmarks of the same reading standard for third, fourth, and fifth graders focus on anticipating the writer's purpose; using context clues; formulating questions; differentiating among multiple meanings; interpreting synonyms, antonyms, and word relationships; summarizing; and synthesizing information in various formats.

Like language, vision is a developmental and learned process. We are born with the equipment necessary for sight; we just haven't learned how to use it yet. The retina and brain must learn how to connect to make sense of the world. This time-sensitive process begins at birth, with our initiation to shapes, patterns, and shadows. Our first view of the world is, literally, black and white with shades of gray. As we mature, the world of color unfolds. Brightly colored mobiles, hung above the crib, catch the attention of infants, encouraging them to focus on the colors and track the movement of the objects. Babies are equally fascinated by their parents' faces and captivated by the movement of their own hands. Studying these features builds connections that teach the eye to focus, to ascertain depth of field, and to synchronize eye movements for visual tracking. Over time babies hone their eye and hand coordination as well as gain a sense of perception and space (Wichita Vision Development Center 2008).

Children also learn how to interpret the emotional state of a character through the image of a smiling face and the mood of a story setting through the shadowy and muted tones of an illustration. They watch an attractive, stylishly clad young actor on a television commercial sip a power drink while maneuvering a designer skateboard, process these images as "desirable," and beg their parents to buy that particular brand of beverage. We have established that today's children take in and respond to visual messages. The challenge is guiding students so that they will become savvy interpreters who are able to create and apply images that communicate symbolism, theme, metaphor, and genre.

Seeing Symbolically

Once my students and I mastered the bits and bytes of taking a digital photograph, understood more about the relationship of the camera to the computer, and gained familiarity with the interactive capabilities of the software we had on hand, we were able to turn our minds to the next question in our quest for visual literacy: How can I create meaning with my images?

Having addressed the processes of taking good photos, we turned our attention to digital manipulations that would allow us to add further depth to our photos. We had, at that time, Microsoft Photo Editor, which provided a cropping feature, a handful of photo filters, and some tools to adjust the hue and saturation of colors. Later, we would add Adobe Photoshop Elements to our collection of software, which greatly expanded our ability to communicate visually. I freely admit that our first forays into digital manipulation were more experimental than intentional, but we quickly realized the creative and communicative possibilities of this visual tool. (See Can You See It? Digital Filters for more details about using digital filters.)

CAN YOU SEE IT? DIGITAL FILTERS

Traditional photographers—the kind who use film—sometimes position filters in front of their camera lenses to add special effects, such as giving an image a glow, softening the edges, or changing the color cast. Digital filters do the same things—and a whole lot more—with the click of a mouse. Digital filters can transform ordinary photographs into expressive works of art.

We began experimenting with Microsoft Photo Editor (now replaced by the folks at Microsoft with Office Picture Manager), which included a small range of filter selections. We experienced an explosion of visual creativity when we began to use Adobe Photoshop Elements. This software includes brush strokes and textured and stylized filters, which make the artistic possibilities limitless. You can transform a photograph into a moody watercolor print or an edgy poster-style drawing with one stroke.

> Again, this is a program that works in layers. The original photograph forms the bottom layer. A filter can be added to the top to form a second layer. And, yes, filters can be layered upon one another, creating some truly unique and moody effects. Your students will enthusiastically explore the scope and range of this expressive tool.

Digital filters enabled students to express their increasingly sophisticated visual literacy skills. For example, nine-year-old Julie used a red filter to take a portrait of her horse, Ruby. "The filter gives you a hint about my horse's name," she explained. Ten-year-old Matthew, whose father restores and resells antique tractors, used a range of filters to reflect the passage of time in his photo series entitled "Tractors Yesterday, Today, and Tomorrow" (see Figures 2.4a, b, and c).

Aubree, a fourth grader, used photo filters in an ambitious photo collection called "Three Sisters." Aubree articulately explained what she learned about visual messaging this way: "Using [digital] filters adds information and details that tell you more about the [subject of the] photograph—personality, ideas, and style behind the person, place, or pet." We were learning that we could craft images to communicate specific ideas, just as we were learning to craft words for the same purpose.

How Can We Show What We Know?

We began to look at the elements of literature and investigate ways to interpret those elements visually. One of our first projects dealt with the writer's tool of symbolism. In her book *Crossing Jordan*, author Adrian Fogelin uses symbolism to communicate her characters' relationships, motives, and beliefs. A fence, a knothole, and a tag-team relay take on deeper meaning within the context of this powerful book about race relations. I challenged a group of fourth graders to create photographs to symbolize the relationship between the two main characters of the story. Digital filters played an important part in this project when students manipulated photographs with the intent of communicating or emphasizing the idea behind the image. We used what we had learned about text overlay and font style

Figures 2.4a, b, and c
Thoughtful use of digital filters, including chalk and charcoal, watercolor, and glow, enabled Matthew to evoke a sense of passing time in his photo essay, "Tractors: Yesterday, Today, and Tomorrow."

Figure 2.5 Using digital filters, students symbolize the relationship between the main characters in *Crossing Jordan*.

and took the project a step further with math and measurement requirements. After printing (we had purchased a color printer by this time, using the proceeds from a school book fair) the students' book jackets, we placed them on our class set of soft-cover books (see Figure 2.5).

This project led us on a visual hunt through our media center's collection of books. Because our library spanned many decades, we were able to find several different editions of many titles.

"What is this book cover suggesting?" I asked, holding up a hardcover book with a period etching on the front.

"That it's for *girls*!" Kyle responded quickly, eyeing the pink gingham cover of *Little House on the Prairie* (Wilder).

"You can't always tell," said a skeptical Kaitlyn. "When we had to read *Hatchet* [Paulsen], I wasn't very excited, but I said I would try it. It turned out to be a great story! Now I know for sure that you can't always judge a book by its cover."

That very first group project established a structure for problem-based learning that we would use many times over. With a work of literature at the center of the process, we would read, research, write, photograph, and digitally manipulate visual information to address questions that began with the phrase "How can I show . . . ?"

We would use the theme of book covers again as we studied genres of literature. By this time, with the addition of Adobe Photoshop Elements software, we used a composite technique to build images in layers and fuse those layers in a finished product. That meant that students could take photographs of each other; place those photos on any background; add text, shapes, and icons; resize the background; and use many types of filters within one image. With these tools, students' visual representations increased dramatically in depth and nuance. Many of their creations now featured the students themselves.

Persuasive writing is part of our fifth-grade language arts curriculum. We investigated the role of persuasive writing in advertising and promotion and linked it to our discussion on book covers.

"Think about the way you browse the shelves. What is it that attracts you to a particular book?" I asked the class.

We developed a list: the cover image, the colors of the cover, the title, the work of a particular author, the summary, and personal tastes in literature. Next, we analyzed the blurbs printed on the book jacket.

"Nothing actually says 'Read This Book!'" observed Samantha. "Okay," I agreed, "but the purpose of the summary is to persuade you to want to read the book. How do the writers do it?"

We devised a second list, which we ambitiously entitled, How to Lure Readers in One Dynamic Paragraph.

1 Keep the language exciting—use the best words.
2 Create a feeling of emotion with your words.
3 Leave some unanswered questions—make them want to read the book to find out what happens.
4 Remember your audience—write on their level.
5 Appeal to personal tastes—let your writing reflect the genre.

With these self-established guidelines in hand, students next selected a genre of literature, created an imaginary book title within that genre, and developed a book cover and written summary of the imaginary book.

We knew before we began this project that there would be many outcomes. The development of a rubric would keep each student focused and on track. The framework for the imagery was broad, giving the students opportunities to apply and sometimes discover technological skills in the creative problem solving necessary for this project. It was fascinating to observe them taking ownership of their visual solutions.

Within the context of illustration and literature, writing drives the imagery, and not the other way around. We began in the same fashion, with each student selecting a favorite genre, and then creating a body of persuasive writing around that choice. Thesaurus skills and peer mentoring came into play as students worked to craft sentences and select words to draw in their readers.

"I'm using a lot of questions in my writing," explained April, "because my story is a mystery—and that's always about finding answers to the clues and questions."

Brandi chose to create a story in the Drama/Tragedy category. Delightfully entitled "A Woman and Her Horse," the story recounts the separation of a girl from her beloved horse, Bakira.

Jory selected the science fiction genre and used a photo of his sister in a tunnel slide as inspiration for his mysteriously eerie story, "The Bubble Trap."

Jackie, a huge fan of J. K. Rowling's Harry Potter fantasies, cast herself as both the protagonist and the antagonist of her imaginary story line.

Summaries written and refined, the children turned their attention to the visual portion of the project. "The words and pictures have to go together, or the whole thing doesn't work!" declared Jackie. And she was right.

Adobe Photoshop Elements allowed the thoughtful application of skills, color choices, filters, fonts, layers of imaging, and layout. This worked hand in hand with the students' summaries to create a whole product. Students developed their own How can I show . . . ? questions. For Brandi, the question was "How can I show sorrow and hope?" For Jory, the question was "How can I show suspense and fear?" Each solution was unique. April centered her visual solution in a thoughtfully staged photograph. Jory made heavy use of filters, cropping, and font selection (see Figure 2.6a). Brandi and Jackie created composite photos, incorporating both original and stock photography (see Figure 2.6b for Brandi's results).

46

On an unusual day, Jory and his sister take a walk in the forest. Suddenly, Jory's sister, Kadyn, disappears. Jory searches for her. He hears something, and runs over to find that his sister is stuck inside a giant bubble! How will Kadyn get out? Who put her there in the first place? Is she going to live? Read the story to find the answers in this science fiction thriller.

A Woman and Her Horse is about the connection that humans have with their animals. When Brandi has to move, it breaks her heart, because her mom says that she cannot take her horse, Bakira. When it is time to part, Brandi says goodbye to Bakira forever. She cries all the way to her new house, and refuses to call it a home without Bakira. There has to be a way to get her back! Brandi won't rest until she and Bakira are together again. Read this drama to see how Brandi and Bakira's love for each other brings them together again.

Figures 2.6a and b As students learn to use the tools of visual literacy, they develop strategies to layer, resize, place, and create unified images and text.

The completed photos and summaries were presented in the PowerPoint format. The power of persuasive imagery and text was reinforced as students from other classes viewed the work, tried to ascertain the genre of the stories and images, voted on whether or not they would want to read that book, and defended their decisions.

PARTNERSHIP WITH PURPOSE

Collaboration is a repetitive theme in this book. Born of necessity—when you have a handful of computers and a class full of students, shared learning becomes part of the experience—it has evolved into the way that we choose to work together at our school. Most teachers would be quick to agree that one-to-one student-computer ratio is the ideal, but less than one-fourth of America's school districts achieve that goal ("Technology Counts" 2008). The rest of us work with what we have—perhaps a computer lab, or maybe just a row of computers in the back of a classroom. Daily we confront the challenge of making the most of the resources at hand.

In our rural school, we use a variety of learning scenarios to maximize our resources—small-group learning, whole-group projects where a team of students learn a skill and then pay it forward to fellow classmates, after-school programs, and some scheduled slots during the school day for independent learning. Our small size—about 220 students in kindergarten through grade five—and low mobility rate offer some advantages, including the opportunity to work with the same students consistently and scaffold their skills over several years.

Is this approach to learning confined to the small school? Of course not. Though everything we know about education tells us that small schools work (Jimerson 2006), shrinking education dollars have resulted in "big box" schools, believed to be more cost efficient. Resourceful teachers, administrators, and families are working hand in hand, in institutions of every configuration and population, to encourage small learning communities within schools—through innovative scheduling, academies, multiage classrooms, and reduced class sizes. Mentoring, small interest groups, and academic inquiry clubs, often fueled by community participation, promote a more intimate environment for personalized learning.

Our classroom teachers bring their students into the media center at least once a week and work side by side with me. The intimate environment of our small school community is especially valuable in this context. Rarely a day goes by when I do not see and talk with nearly every teacher on campus. Those encounters identify areas of need—for both materials and training—that enable our school media clerk, Becky Blankenship, to assemble book-bag collections to deliver to various classrooms and that help me prepare lessons to strengthen and extend the curricula. Our collaborative efforts also extend beyond the regular school schedule; teachers often come to the media center after hours to learn new technology skills and plan multidisciplinary lessons. (An added incentive for spending time together is gaining credit toward state recertification requirements.)

It is very encouraging to see teachers integrate their new skills back into the classroom. For example, first-year teacher Carrie Pedri created a magical interdisciplinary unit on the culture and history of India after participating in a series of after-school visual literacy workshops. Her third graders collaborated on a digital retelling of Rudyard Kipling's *Rikki-tikki-tavi*. Sometimes teachers will request additional coaching after viewing students' media projects. Chris DeRosier, teaching a combination class of third and fourth graders, was inspired after viewing a student media project on food chains to develop his own classroom collection of digital stories on biomes and food webs. Felice Freeman, a first-grade teacher, collaborated with me to create an electronic research project about spiders.

We start engaging this eye generation in kindergarten, cultivating simple skills in technology, language arts, research, and critical and creative thinking; then we expand students' knowledge as they progress through the elementary grades. We discuss, analyze, and create various methods of sharing information. We communicate visually and textually, discovering how to "read" information in divergent formats. We integrate new skills over the years. These students expect to be engaged in active learning that links traditional education to new technology tools. They are fully engaged in the hard work of rigorous, creative, interdisciplinary learning. And they are having a great time.

Josh, a fifth grader, expressed it this way: "When you're learning like this, you don't realize you're learning. You think you're just having fun. But, later on, you realize you *were* learning. And, you know, it feels good!

Breaking a project into a series of tasks—research, writing, storyboarding, technology application, presentation, evaluation—lends itself to the establishment of small learning communities within a classroom and stretches the impact of the available tools. Thoughtful pairing of students encourages the twenty-first-century learning skills of teamwork, critical thinking, and creative problem solving. While each student ultimately produces his or her own work, adhering to the philosophy that two heads are better than one allows students to share what they know, discover solutions as a team, and support, rather than compete.

"How can I show the collision of cultures?" was the central question behind a project centered on themes of resolution and conflict in *The People of Sparks* by Jeanne DuPrau. Up to this point in our collaboration, the students and I had been concentrating on combining digitally altered photos and text into a single image. We had designed our projects to convey a concept through a single image. Now we wanted to expand our work so that a sequence of images could show the progression of ideas and actions—What happens? And what happens next?—and build the foundation for digital storytelling.

We also were experimenting to find new applications for computer software programs. Occasionally I will set aside time for students to engage in playful learning because I believe that self-discovery is an important component of mastering technology. As teachers, we are often so task oriented and time pressed that we forget to make space for experimentation, wonder, failure, and the communication of ideas that make learning personal and meaningful. So periodically I ask students to spend about twenty minutes exploring a particular software program, with the goal of discovering a new feature, devising a plan to integrate the knowledge with previous skills, and sharing their findings with the rest of the group. During one exploration, several students discovered the shape tool in Adobe Photoshop Elements. Students were electrified by the peer-to-peer demonstration of how this "talk-balloon" feature could be incorporated into their photographic displays, similar to the way comic-strip artists give their characters voice.

Students already knew how to move and resize objects and text and quickly realized the possibilities of moving and reshaping symbols and icons into their work. Their interest grew when we found a set of graphic history books recently added to our school collection. The students were fascinated by the cartoon versions of Lincoln's presidency (Olson 2005), the landing of the Mayflower (Lassieur 2006), and the Salem witch trials (Martin 2005). These influences were evident in the students' work; nearly all chose to create a sequence of events in cartoon format.

Was the similarity a bad thing? It was certainly different from previous projects, where each outcome was markedly unique. After reflecting, I realized that the near-unanimous selection of a single format was typical of the way children gain familiarity with a skill. It also suggested the creative collaboration that this generation of students has grown accustomed to. They want to do whatever their peers can do. And when someone discovers a new feature of technology, others want to practice it and put it to use right away.

Teachers aren't so different. We often read about a new learning modality and seek to integrate it into our classrooms. We might learn how to make a digital slide show, create a newsletter with publishing software, or build a web log with Blogger, and suddenly our lessons blossom with technology applications. We learn something new and experiment with ways to make that knowledge work for us. It is a reflection of our growth, as people, as students, and as teachers.

We Get the Picture

The People of Sparks examines the ethical, practical, and cultural problems that arise when two distinctly different societies collide. It did not take long for my fifth-grade students to come up with a list of historical examples of this phenomenon, and to realize that *resolution* can mean many things. It is a concept with myriad viewpoints. The theme of this story suggested partnering students to create a sequence of imagery. Students had arrived at that crux of mastery and understanding, moving from task-oriented technology applications to the making of personal decisions about what they would use and how they would apply it. They knew how to manipulate and layer images and were comfortable with a wide range of tools that

Figures 2.7a and b Ana and Angel developed a series of images to portray the evolution of the relationship between the societies of Ember and Sparks.

allowed them to make those applications. They integrated photography, icons, and fonts. They made judicious use of space, perspective, and color to communicate. It was very exciting for me to observe their work in progress. Their "show-me" solutions yielded some of the most sophisticated and imaginative visual imagery to date (see Figures 2.7a and b).

DuPrau's story line is configured on the premise that two isolated societies converge. Long accustomed to widely agreed-upon viewpoints, neither can comprehend, or accept, the perceptions of the new society. Each is "boxed in" by long-standing, culturally inherent beliefs.

Angel and Ana worked as a team to show how cultures collide. As we examine their work, we notice that they used icons from the story to identify the subjects. A smudge on Angel's cheek identifies her as a hardworking member of the agrarian society of Sparks. The body language and facial expressions of each subject speak of disagreement, division, and narrow perceptions. They used color selection to identify the cultures; pinks and purples represent the dominant society of Sparks, while the community of Ember is represented by blues. The dominance or balance of a particular color palette indicates the shift of power between the cultures. A clever phrase, with dual meaning, is artistically displayed; each letter is boxed with clues that suggest the conflict between the groups. Thoughtful layering of images confines the citizen of Sparks to one side of the image, and the citizen of Ember to the other. The girls developed a composite image that is clearly and literally divided.

Another pair of students incorporated apple- and egg-shaped icons into their visual representation of the resolution of these cultures. I admit that I was skeptical about the degree of thoughtfulness behind this inclusion in the team's visual solution—those icons were just so much fun—but it seems I had underestimated my students. When the time came for the team to present and explain their work to the group, the deliberation behind their choices was clear.

"The apple is a symbol of all of the things that Sparks has and Ember doesn't have," explained Cierra quietly. "The apple is fresh. No one in Ember even knows what fresh fruit is. Fruit is the end of the cycle after a tree grows from a seed. The apple is bright red. Everything in Ember is dusty and brown. "And," she added "you give an apple to someone—like your teacher—to show them that you like them."

"Eggs probably look like rocks to the people of Ember," added Brandi, "but they are filled with life inside. And both things are part of a cycle of growing. They start out looking like one thing, but end up being something completely different."

Their "simple" solution was, marvelously, filled with intent. The symbols they chose reflected their real lives as children in a rural farming community. Cierra and Brandi effectively translated the big ideas from the story into a world of symbolic meaning easily understood by the other children. Clearly, I stood corrected.

54

CHAPTER THREE

Reshowing and Retelling Stories

The illiterate of the 21st century will not be those who cannot read
and write, but those who cannot learn, unlearn, and relearn.
—Alvin Toffler, *The Third Wave*

When we embrace the notion that *how* we teach is as relevant to the learn-ing process as *what* we teach, we naturally begin to expand our instruc-tion to address a wider range of learning styles and literacies. We continue to work within traditional disciplines, but our approach to teaching those disciplines broadens. The inclusion of art, technology, and imagery adds power to traditional tools such as books, paper, and pencils. Our students become actively engaged in visual, auditory, and kinesthetic interpretation and production of information. As we reach into their world, we transform the everyday business of teaching and learning into a shared, creative jour-ney.

Teaching within a framework of language arts, science, social studies, or any other discipline, while embedding both traditional and visual literacy strategies, enables us to add breadth and depth to the skills that students use to analyze and communicate meaning. This may sound ambitious, espe-cially at the elementary level, but it keeps learning exciting while meeting a multiplicity of standards, literacies, and modalities. And the fluid nature of this instruction encourages students to make vital connections among basic skills, abstract concepts, and real-life applications.

Let's examine this approach through the lens of visual storytelling. Sequencing is one of the most basic and essential of communication skills, integral to everything from decoding simple words to creating and express-ing complex ideas through text and images. Teachers have long relied on sequencing—the "retelling" of stories in the proper order—as a tool to measure students' comprehension. Children must master this skill to make sense of texts or to create their own. The visual expression of sequencing comes into play as students use imagery to represent, convey, and extend the progression of ideas. In the following section, I will explain how I introduce this basic skill to younger students, build on students' knowledge of sequencing as they mature, use more complex techniques to stimulate higher-order thinking skills, and, finally, guide learners toward expressing their understanding in various modalities.

PUTTING THE "SEE" INTO SEQUENCING

In Western cultures, we read, write, and decode information from left to right. Yet curiously, curriculum in the elementary grades rarely touches on left to right scanning, perhaps assuming that children have an intrinsic ability to learn this process. That faulty assumption can interfere with children's comprehension, says Dr. Marion Blank (1983), director of A Light on Literacy program at Columbia University. For example, the letters *R*, *A*, and *T* reflect very different meanings, depending on the way we sequence them:

R+A+T = RAT
T+A+R = TAR
A+R+T = ART

Blank reminds us that in teaching our youngest learners to make sense of letters, words, and images, we must provide explicit instruction about left to right sequencing. Visual connections are particularly helpful when showing students how to recognize the sequential elements of a story. Interestingly, even traditional left to right, top to bottom reading is being affected by the digital age. Recent studies indicate that today's youngsters read more information from their computer screens than they do from the printed page. This shift is transforming a generation of methodical readers into scanners. Eye-tracking studies show that younger readers tend to pick up information in an E or F shape: taking in the banner of a web page, scanning the navigation bar, and glancing through the images and hyperlinks before they decide whether or not they want to read the page (Poynter Institute for Media Studies 2007).

Typically teachers will pause frequently when reading aloud to ask students, "What do you think will happen next?" We use this question to encourage children to predict events based on their understanding of the story. But I have found that many students need additional clues before they are able to recall, retell, and make inferences about text.

I now use several tools to help my youngest students "see" sequencing and interpret story patterns (see Can You See It? Story Patterns for more information). The simplest of these tools include illustrations that tell the story visually. Books in the Dorling Kindersley's Readers series are particularly good props because they integrate simple text and photographs beautifully. One of my favorite books in this series is Karen Wallace's *Born to Be a Butterfly*. After I read the book to students, I distribute some of the prominent images, copied and reinforced with cardstock.

Through discussion and collaboration, the students rearrange the images until they can agree on the correct chronological order of the butterfly's metamorphosis. Rereading the story helps them evaluate their accuracy, clarify their choices, and make any necessary adjustments in their visual representation.

Other stories require more sophisticated architecture. To help students see the multidimensional foundation of cumulative stories, I cut out a series of laminated concentric circles that we can write and rewrite on with dry-erase markers. When I pull out these circles after reading a story, students know they will be asked to rebuild the sequence. Classic folk tales, such as *The House That Jack Built* and *I Know an Old Lady Who Swallowed a Fly*, work well for this approach. Using the laminated circles to reconstruct the plot structure, we start with the smallest object (such as the fly in *I Know an Old Lady Who Swallowed a Fly*) and work our way up to the horse, of course. In this way, students discover how text and images work together to build a story as well as how the same story can be viewed, organized, and communicated from multiple perspectives.

Other story patterns reveal themselves through the physical weaving and reweaving of story elements within a particular rhythm. For example, a student who holds the repetitive phrase from Elizabeth Spurr's *The Long, Long Letter* will find him- or herself physically moving down the story line to interject the repetitive phrase as the story unfolds.

Kinesthetic story patterning can result in some pretty intricate footwork, as in the story of *Epossumondas* by Colleen Salley. The main character, a baby opossum, follows directions exactly and hilariously—but applies these directions to subsequent, not previous, circumstances. There is much laughter, furrowing of brows, and spirited discussion among the students as they figure out how to "circle back" and rearrange the story elements to illustrate the interlocking pattern of this Deep South tale.

CAN YOU SEE IT? STORY PATTERNS

Literary patterns enable emergent readers, who may not yet be able to decode a wide range of individual words, to participate and "read along" by predicting and identifying the sequence of a story. These widely used storytelling tools encourage fluency, inflection, and emotion in oral reading. These same patterns are effective for building writing skills. The following list shows various types of literary patterns along with a book that exemplifies each pattern.

Characterization patterns establish marked traits in a central character that enable readers to predict episode outcomes. (*Amelia Bedelia* by Peggy Parish)

Chronological patterns reveal a time sequence and order for the unfolding of events. (*The Grouchy Ladybug* by Eric Carle)

Cultural patterns build on an information sequence such as the calendar, seasons, time, the alphabet, or a number line. (*Chicken Soup with Rice* by Maurice Sendak)

Cumulative, or building, patterns echo a previous portion of a story, but add a new part. (*Bringing the Rain to Kapiti Plain* by Verna Aardema)

Interlocking patterns tell a story in which each part relates to the previ-

ous in a predictable way. (*Five Chinese Brothers* by Claire Hutchet
Bishop)

Problem/Solution patterns center on an issue and the progression of
ideas that leads to a solution. (*The Three Little Javelinas* by Susan
Lowell)

Repetitive patterns use duplicative phrases or ideas throughout a story.
(*A Fine, Fine School* by Sharon Creech)

Rhythm and rhyme patterns unfold through a predictable cadence
that becomes familiar to readers. (*Seven Little Monsters* by Maurice
Sendak)

As previously mentioned, stories can be revealed through imagery as well as
text. Author David Wiesner demonstrates his genius as a visual storyteller
through his book *Tuesday*. This cleverly developed story, communicated
entirely through Wiesner's illustrations, recounts the remarkable events
of a seemingly ordinary evening. Students "read" the story through visual
and sequential analysis. The website where Wiesner explains the creative
process behind *Tuesday* (http://www.houghtonmifflinbooks.com/authors/
wiesner/process/process.shtml) thoughtfully integrates imagery, text, and
conversation to show the evolution of the book from concept to storyboard
to completed product. The detailed explanation provides an excellent model
for students as they learn how to bring their own visual stories to life.

Reading, Reconfiguring, and Representing

Usually in second grade, my students begin to use more sophisticated
sequencing strategies to understand how the various components of a
story contribute to the whole. We play a little game called "Stir Me a Story"
to illustrate the synergy. Using teacher-made cardboard cutouts of eggs,
butter, flour, sugar, three baking pans, a mixing bowl, and a decorated
cake, we analyze the parts of a story. Each ingredient represents a different element: The flour is the setting, the eggs are the characters, and so
forth. Once we have mixed up the "batter," we divide it among three pans,
respectively labeled *beginning*, *middle*, and *end*. The students craft single

sentences to recap the plot. For *The Three Little Pigs* (Galdone), the students might offer oral descriptions such as:

> "Three small pigs decided to go out on their own and wanted to build their own houses in the country."
> "They were followed by a bad wolf that destroyed the weakest houses and tried to eat the pigs."
> "The last pig, which built the strongest house, played a trick on the wolf so that he would leave them alone."

Putting those sentences together, in the proper sequence, teaches students to summarize, a skill they will use many times in future grades.

When we review the ingredients in our "cake," we find that we have developed within the three sentences information that helps us understand the setting, the characters, the problem, and the solution, as well as the beginning, the middle, and the end. Because *The Three Little Pigs* belongs to the genre of fairy tales, we can go a bit further and analyze the story graphically.

Fairy tales share similar story elements. Events tend to happen in threes. The theme of good versus evil is often represented. Fairy tales usually include fantasy or magic. And, of course, they end "happily ever after." We use these indicators to analyze stories and determine if they meet the requirements for a fairy tale.

The transformation of story elements into visual formats links directly to student writing. The comprehension tools that we use when analyzing a story—including sequencing, summarizing, and identifying the parts in relation to the whole—provide a blueprint for students to follow as they build their own stories.

Beginning writers often get flummoxed when they try to add details or change the order of events after the first draft of their ideas. To be sure, computer word-processing software makes this task much easier than in the old days of scratching out or erasing scribbles and rewriting every version from beginning to end. But young children need a visual reference for understanding how to shape and rearrange text. Returning the technology term *cut and paste* to its traditional roots can give students a hands-on method of exploring the process of writing and revising stories.

Figure 3.1   Jon makes some final decisions about the sequence of his story entitled "Fun on My Farm."

I ask kindergarten and first graders to choose a topic of personal interest and write a short story on wide-ruled paper. They use scissors to cut the story into a series of sentences, which they can physically move around to shift the sequence and edit or insert new ideas into the story line. (I'll return to this type of project in Chapter 4 when discussing visual connections to research in K–5 classrooms.) When they are satisfied with their work, students use glue sticks to place their sentences permanently onto legal-sized paper. Visual sequencing comes into play when students create images for each part of their stories and then match their artwork to their text (see Figure 3.1).

Simple computer software programs, such as Easybook by Sunburst, help students create a finished product in traditional book form (see Can You See It? Book Builders). These book-publishing software programs introduce the technological processes that students will need to know as they move deeper into the creative world of digital storytelling.

CAN YOU SEE IT? BOOK BUILDERS

An original story, complementary images, a few simple materials, and some creative brainpower are all the materials students need to construct a book. Handmade books can be as original and artistic as the stories themselves. Susan Kapuscinski Gaylord's website, Making Books (http://www.makingbookswithchildren.blogspot.com), has a wealth of creative options for developing books of various forms and materials. This artist/teacher even includes how-to videos on her site.

It is sometimes helpful to have a template from which to work, especially if you are producing a large number of handmade books. Easybook and Easybook Deluxe (http://store.sunburst.com/) provide an easy and affordable format for creating books that include spaces on each page for imagery and text. I especially like the choices within the program because they accommodate a wide range of ages and learners. Our youngest students create accompanying images on paper presized to fit nicely within the context of Easybook. This helps them gain familiarity with the format. Over time, as students become proficient with typing and technology skills, they begin to use the program independently.

If you are dealing with mass production and prolific writers, ready-bound books are available. McGraw-Hill offers ready-to-write books in a variety of sizes, such as a seven-by-ten-inch format with sixteen blank pages. You can purchase these Blank Books for Young Authors through many educational supply vendors.

To learn more about writing with young children, take a look at *Talking, Drawing, and Writing* by Martha Horn and Mary Ellen Giacobbe (2007).

With the pressure to raise test scores at every level of education, we don't often hear the word *developmental* mentioned in schools these days. But I like to think that the scaffolding of skills and activities described here would make Piaget proud. As students learn and apply the skill of sequencing through concrete, kinesthetic activities, they are challenged to link "doing" with "thinking" about reading and writing. The physical and visual connections, in turn, prepare children to understand abstract ideas that can be artfully and intelligently expressed through technology.

SHOW ME A STORY

Each year the administrators, faculty, and parents in our school community discuss learning goals and develop strategies to reach those goals in the form of a school improvement plan. Expanding students' knowledge of science is a primary focus of our current school plan. To enhance the second graders' study of biological food chains, my teaching colleagues consulted me about a multimedia project that would incorporate research, technology, science, and literacy.

We decided to embark on a journey into digital storytelling. We wanted students to extend their classroom study of food chains through research and use the information they gathered to develop creative nonfiction narratives. They would be able to use imagery and audio components to complement the text and create a communication fusion of words, symbols, music, and sound effects.

I first learned about digital storytelling in 2005 when I attended a workshop presented by Deborah Hargroves, an elementary media specialist from Savannah, Georgia. Deborah kindly offered advice when I returned to my school and started putting some of her ideas into practice. *DigiTales*, Bernajean Porter's (2005) comprehensive book about digital storytelling, filled in other gaps for me.

For those of us who grew up glued to the printed page, digital media can sound mighty complicated. We may envision Hollywood editing rooms, expensive equipment, and sensory skills that only talented artists possess. I'm living proof that these barriers can be bypassed. We can achieve excellent results everyday in ordinary classrooms with the help of a few accessible tools. My digital storytelling laboratory includes a Kodak EasyShare Camera (affordable, extremely child-friendly, and practically unbreakable), a computer, a fifteen-dollar microphone that plugs into the computer, and Adobe Photoshop Elements and Premiere software. I also have a CD-ROM of copyright-free music (see Can You See It? Copy Right! for more information) called SoundzAbound (http://www.soundzabound.com), purchased at an education conference.

CAN YOU SEE IT? COPY RIGHT!

As classroom teachers, we set the tone for cultivating respect for authorship. Copyright laws exist to protect a wide range of materials—books, photos, audio clips, architecture, choreography, websites, and more. Here's the good news: copyright law makes many exceptions for educational institutions. Sound recordings and audio clips may be used in multimedia projects produced by either teachers or students, as long as the project has an educational purpose, stays within the confines of the school community, and is a not-for-profit project. Of course, it is vital to credit the source and let viewers know where they might be able to find that audio for purchase. It's also a good idea to let the viewing audience know why and how a particular audio selection adds meaning to the corresponding images and narration. Many school districts adhere to the 10 percent rule: that is, no more than 10 percent of a recording may be incorporated into a multimedia project.

There are a couple of excellent sources for gaining familiarity with the parameters and possibilities of copyright. The Copyright Management Center at Purdue University (http://www.copyright.iupui.edu/quickguide.htm) offers up-to-the-minute information on this topic. Arizona State University (http://library.west.asu.edu/subjects/edu/copyrighttutorial.html) provides a teacher-friendly tutorial through the library site.

Copyright free is a beautiful phrase. That means that the material is part of the public domain and may be freely accessed and used in projects. When surfing the Internet for copyright-free music sources, look for the phrases copyright free, royalty free, public domain, or free play.

These simple tools enable students to design high-quality digital media projects, which fuse the science, technology, communications, and social interaction skills that are essential for twenty-first-century learning (Digital Media Alliance Florida, www.dmaflorida.org/). A key part of this process is convergence—the blending of information and skills through applied learning. We want our students to provide evidence that they understand the relationships among visual, textual, and verbal sources of information through a product that combines reading, writing, research, and speaking skills. We want them to create and communicate collaboratively. In this particular case, we also want them to learn more about the marine food chain because the core subject is science. Finally, we want their work to have a purpose beyond completing the teacher's assignment. For example, their digital stories become teaching tools; a local marine science education center uses them as part of a community education program.

Keeping in mind the skills students have previously mastered, I take quick stock of what they still need to learn. My intent is to build on what they already know. In kindergarten and first grade, the students learned how to use a digital camera. They also discovered how authors link their ideas to create a sequence of information. As second graders they will move from whole-group to small-group collaboration to develop their own story sequences. Although the students have some familiarity with computers, they will be learning the new skills of saving and retrieving digital pictures to and from a folder. For the first time, the students will build pictures in layers, combining text and symbols with imagery. I have already demonstrated how to sort and sequence slides; now they will work through this process independently.

The students' digital stories usually include an audio narrative, music, and imagery presented in a slide-show format. Video clips and sound effects can be created and inserted into the story line. Student-friendly software programs such as Microsoft PowerPoint or Photo Story or Adobe Photoshop Elements bring all the elements of a digital story together nicely. Some software programs, such as Adobe Premiere Elements, offer special effects that enable students to pan and zoom within a slide. Some enable students to overlay visual, textual, and symbolic forms of information. The linear nature of a slide show aligns perfectly with the story and sequencing skills that students have used in the more traditional learning activities of reading and writing books.

From Plankton to People: Dinner in the Deep Blue Sea

These second-grade students are creating a digital story as an enrichment and extension of their classroom science study of marine food chains. Because our students live on the Atlantic coast, they draw on personal and general knowledge of their environment as they explore the subject in more detail. Their prior experience with story sequencing helps them understand how to design a pattern of events, with the next largest predator in the food chain consuming the one before it in the story. In addition to their science studies, these second graders have already done some independent reading on the subject. Grade-appropriate selections within our school collection include:

- *What Are Food Chains and Food Webs?* by Bobbie Kalman and Jacqueline Langille
- *Who Eats What?* by Patricia Lauber
- *Food Chains* by Peter Riley
- *Barnacles Eat with Their Feet* by Sherry Shehan

We begin to talk about our digital stories.

"Plankton are at the bottom of the food chain," declares Jessica, "and I want to learn about them."

"Okay," I respond. "If plankton are at the bottom of the food chain, what is at the top?" The students suggest a range of possibilities, largely based on the size of the marine life. We talk about sharks, whales, and manatees, and go to the Internet together to learn more about where these creatures fit into the food chain.

These coastal children, all of whom have been fishing, floundering, or shrimping at one time or another, begin to discuss the possibility that humans belong at the top of the food chain. They engage in spirited discussion, with some students arguing that humans are not truly marine creatures. They ultimately decide to place humans at the top of the food chain, but reserve the right to expand and redirect the story as they continue to develop it.

With plankton holding up one end of our food chain, and humans holding the other, the students are faced with the task of filling in the blanks. They use the Internet and a simple research technique, which involves typing the name of the marine animal under the search term *predator*. Through research and collaboration, the students envision a likely food chain: Squids, crabs, sea turtles . . . the list grows. I supplement their work by locating age-appropriate books on the topic and previewing Internet sites that they might consult for further research.

"Last week, we came up with a progression of animals that might make up a marine food chain," I explain during our next class session. "We put plankton at one end of the food chain and human beings at the other. You came up with a list of animals that might be part of a marine food chain. What do we need to know about each of these creatures in order to develop a story?"

The ideas begin to fly. We need to know what the creatures eat. We need to know what they look like. We need to be sure that they live in the same ocean, and in the same part of that ocean. And we need to be sure that the food chain we formulated during our last meeting is accurate. By this time, each student has selected one animal in the proposed chain for individual study. Brandon has a special interest in sea turtles. Christopher wants to learn more about sharks. Tyler is eager to explore squids. Jessica has already staked a claim on plankton, but Kinsey shares her interest so the girls agree to work together.

We have already engaged in some preliminary Internet research. Books provide an important second source, helping students to verify information and elaborate. Each student notes his or her findings on an index card and uses the reverse side to summarize the information through a descriptive paragraph. The children's real-life experience with marine life is evident in their phrasing. One student includes this description: "And along comes a shrimp. He's a nice three-incher!" Ordered sequentially, the note cards form the first draft of our group story.

"What's missing?" I ask the students as we look at their research collectively. Reading their writing aloud helps us evaluate the content and flow. Gabe immediately points out that the story does not tell us how the marine animals come into contact with each other and exactly what happens when they *do*. So we create a list of verbs—*swim, propel, glide, float, catch, crunch, swallow, devour*—and we use these descriptors to connect the information and develop a better narrative flow. The sequence begins to come together as a story. The students are having fun with the process and want to add some humor to the story, so they sprinkle phrases such as "Tasty!" "Watch out!" and "It's lunchtime!" throughout the narrative.

"What if we were going to share this story with a first-grade class?" I ask the students. "They haven't learned about the food chain. What would those students need to know in order to understand this story better?"

"They need to know what a food chain is," volunteers Jessica.

We go back to our original sources to come up with a definition for a food chain, write it on an index card, and put the description at the beginning of our card sequence. Using the lens of a first-grade student, the children reread the story, this time realizing that they also need to define terms such as *predator* and *prey*. They research and add that information to the story.

Something has been bothering Brandon. Our food-chain story is too straightforward and simplistic for his tastes. He wants to include information about the food web. "Like this part," he says, pointing to a portion of the story where a fisherman captures the shark. "Sharks attack and sometimes kill people, too. I think that needs to be part of the story."

Beginning with the phrase, "The food chain can take many turns," we circle back to add nuance to the story. This serves to broaden the concept of a food chain and also satisfies the concern some students had about placing humans at the top of a marine food chain. When we have agreed on the information and sequence of our cards, we quickly number them to keep our ideas in order. The scripted portion of our storyboard is complete.

Now it is time to consider the visual portion of our story. We know that we will be photographing objects that will help us illustrate the sequence of events from our narrative. After suggesting puppets, stuffed animals, drawings, and cartoons as possible ways to visually represent our story, the students eventually opt for a series of paper cutouts that will be displayed on a larger drawing. The paper cutouts can be rearranged any number of ways to indicate predator and prey roles in the food chain and enable the students to quickly set up photos that will become part of our digital storytelling project. This simple, hands-on method of assembling images gives each student a chance to contribute artwork, creativity, and directorial flair to the group project. It also helps me manage the materials for the six classes that I will teach that day.

The students design a background template that includes a cross section of a marine habitat—the ocean floor, a span of ocean, the ocean surface, and a bit of sky. Kinsey and Jessica volunteer to start filling in the scene as we develop our storyboard concepts, adding three leaping dolphins, a few clouds in the sky, and some rocks to anchor the sandy ocean floor.

Meanwhile, their classmates and I review the index cards of sentences and definitions to determine the best sequence for our visual elements. Much of the process seems self-evident to the children. For instance, if a shrimp eats plankton, then both creatures must be featured in the photo that we use to illustrate the action. As they sketch these details onto the background display, the students quickly realize that they will have to collaborate to make sure that the scale of the marine animals correlates to their proportionate size. They come up with a simple solution by cutting watercolor paper into graduating sizes, perhaps in reference to the graduating circles we used in previous lessons to represent the sequence of building stories. The smallest square of the stack of watercolor paper goes to our plankton artists, the largest to Christopher, who will be drawing the shark. As we climb up the food chain, the proposed visuals become more elaborate. Tyler wants to draw a squid with detachable ink. "The ink is an important part of the squid's defense. I want to show that part when he faces his predator."

As our visual story builds to the part where the human and the shark might connect, the students realize that they will need some additional images. Someone volunteers to draw a boat and a net. We now have a list of the visual elements we will use to show our story, and the students use pencils, black markers, crayons, and scissors to create them (see Can You See It? Storyboards for more information on storyboards). The next time we meet, we will be ready to shoot our story.

The following day, applying the digital camera skills acquired in previous projects, the students arrange the visual elements of their story then photograph the images from a bird's-eye view. Of course, each student wants to shoot his or her portion of the story. As one child snaps photographs, another consults the storyboard to be sure that the correct visuals are included. Other students have all of the artwork organized and are

70

acting as impromptu prop masters. There are plenty of art directors on the set as well, offering advice on the placement of each marine creature, the angle of the camera, the parts of the background to crop or include. Editing, revision, and discussion continue to unfurl through the photography process, as the children realize that they may need more than one photo to communicate a sequence of information, such as the sea turtle's pursuit of a squid across the ocean.

We load all of the photos onto the computer and then use a slideshow sorter to rearrange shots, discard some, and form a short list of retakes.

CAN YOU SEE IT? STORYBOARDS

Students quickly embrace the engaging business of creating digital stories, but that creativity can melt into chaos without a road map. Storyboards are the "gotta-have" guide; they provide direction and focus for digital storytellers. These graphic organizers are essentially large comic strips, tying visual and textual information together in a sequential way. They help students figure out where they are going with their stories and offer valuable points of reference throughout the creative process.

Using the storyboard as a tool for review and discussion helps teams to identify parts of their production that are missing or that might need more detail or clarification. It comes in handy once again as they link their photos together in the proper sequence. Adobe Photoshop Elements and Adobe Premiere Elements work hand in hand to help students get, organize, and arrange images sequentially. Finally, the storyboard guides students through the narration of their story, helping them make sure that their imagery and audio are in sync. Storyboards don't have to be fancy—just about anything will do. We find that a series of five-by-seven-inch index cards does the job; the cards can be easily reordered or edited as discussion and collaboration among the students brings new ideas or details to light. Yellow sticky notes are also great for those creative or functional add-ins. Once we get everything just the way we like it, a generous application of tape keeps the plans and details in place. It works for us! But you can download more sophisticated storyboard formats at Schoolhouse video (http://www.schoolhousevideo .org/Pages/Storyboard.pdf).

Want to learn more about storyboarding? Try Karen J. Lloyd's Storyboard Blog (http://karenjlloyd.com/blog/2007/11/13/so-what-is-a-storyboard-anyway/).

The mistakes we make help us refine our skills. For example, the students quickly see that it is easier to get a clearly focused close-up by shooting from a distance of a few feet and then cropping the photo digitally, rather than by trying to find the perfect physical proximity to the subject. We also discover that we will need slides for our story title and credits. Adobe Photoshop Elements and Adobe Premiere Elements, the computer software we have chosen for our project, enable us to add text and symbols to our photographs. The students decide to layer some arrows over certain photographs, such as those depicting the human and the shark, to show that the food chain can move in more than one direction. We also add the words *predator* and *prey* to the picture of the shrimp and crab.

Although we are using a slide show of still photographs, we take advantage of the software's "pan-and-zoom" option, which creates the effect of movement within the slide show and focuses the viewer's attention on particular portions of the image. This software program also has a child-friendly audio component. A simple microphone, plugged into the computer, and the stop and start buttons are all that we need to include audio narrative. A second audio track is available, so we add copyright-free music for extra interest.

"Dinner in the Deep Blue Sea" is ready for its premiere. The entire project has required half a dozen whole-group work sessions of approximately fifty minutes and a short series of partnered mini-sessions for audio recording. This digital story was shared with other students in the school, made a return appearance as a teaching tool during the following school year, and ultimately made its way to our local marine science center, where it is regularly shown as part of the center's student education program. "Dinner in the Deep Blue Sea" was also recognized as a Judge's Choice award winner at the 2007 International Student Media Festival in Anaheim, California.

An added benefit of this project is that students have the option of answering open-response questions on the state's mandated science exams in visual, graphic, or text formats. This project gave them plenty of practice with the various techniques (See Figures 3.2–3.4).

Figure 3.2 These second graders work together as a production team to create, photograph, and sequence images for their story, "Dinner in the Deep Blue Sea."

Figure 3.3 A sample slide from "Dinner in the Deep Blue Sea." Students begin to learn how to layer images with the addition of simple shapes and icons.

Figure 3.4 A desktop computer and plug-in microphone make a fine impromptu sound studio. Here Summer acts as the sound engineer for Nina's narration of a story.

HELPING THEM TELL THEIR STORIES, THEIR WAY

By third grade, students are ready to work through the digital story process much more independently. My role morphs from instructor to advisor as children work with partners to design their own projects. One of our third-grade literature circles has been discussing *The Music of the Dolphins* by Karen Hesse, which is about a feral child raised by a pod of dolphins. The main character, Mila, is later "rescued" and studied by a group of scientists. Mila is a nonspeaker, using instead the only language known to her, the "music of the dolphins," to communicate with the strangely human world in which she finds herself entrapped.

We decide to use the book as a springboard to genre studies that involve digital storytelling. Students use their electronic catalog search skills to locate examples of science fiction, biography, poetry, folk tales, and other genres within our media collection. Working together, they develop criteria for selected genres. For instance, the students realize that stories in the mystery genre always include clues, suspense, unanswered questions, and surprise endings. Nonfiction stories are based on facts. Using the benchmarks they established, the student teams select a genre and begin

to develop a story around the topic of dolphins.

Merry and Josh decide to write a poem about dolphins. Megan and Nur want to create a fantasy story. Ashlyn, Audrey, and Anastaysa choose a documentary piece about the dangers that face dolphins in the wild.

As we examine published examples of poetry, fantasy, nonfiction, and other literary genres, we pay particular attention to imagery. Based on this investigation, Ashlyn, Audrey, and Anastaysa decide to use photographs to illustrate their story, "Dolphin Struggles" (see Figure 3.5). Megan and Nur's "My Day with the Dolphin" becomes a playful personal narrative, based in part on a news article about the discovery of a dolphin with small legs tucked behind its flippers. Megan and Nur take the artistic route, using the cutout figures and background display technique described in the second-grade food-chain project (see Figure 3.6). Merry and Josh deliberate about the best way to illustrate their poetry project. They eventually decide to use stock photos, but to manipulate the images with digital filtering to add "more poetry" to the pictures (see Figures 3.7a, b, c, and d).

Figure 3.5 Ashlyn makes a final revision to her group's storyboard in preparation for the production of a digital documentary, "Dolphin Struggles."

Figure 3.6 Megan and Nur work on the visuals for their digital story, "My Day with the Dolphin."

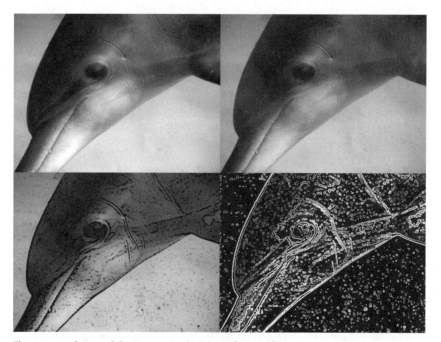

Figures 3.7a, b, c, and d Successive building of photo filters can result in beautiful imagery. This stock photo of a dolphin (courtesy of http://www.freedigitalphotos.net) has been manipulated with the addition of Photoshop Elements filters, including different clouds, poster edges, and glowing edges.

76

I want to add a few words here about the use of photographs in digital stories. Many students take and use original photographs in their digital stories. For example, "Lindsey and Morgan: Two Best Friends" tells the story of a family friendship that goes back several generations. As Lindsey and Morgan planned their story, they developed a list of the photographs they would need, including shots of the girls at school, their parents, the family farms, and so on, all easily accessible subjects for original photography. In contrast, the story "Dolphin Struggles" presented a production challenge for Ashlyn, Audrey, and Anastaysa. They decided to combine original drawings, such as those depicting floating marine trash and a dolphin caught in a fishing net, with selected stock photos, such as a dolphin rescue operation and a wild dolphin pod.

Like published text and music, most photographs are copyrighted and should not be used without permission. However, copyright-free stock photos are available. Be aware that there are creative common license guidelines attached to some online photo sources. If your students are planning to use filters, layer photographs, or crop images, be sure to select a stock photo source that allows students to create derivative images for educational purposes. A little advance investigation will help you find websites that are suitable for young learners. (For a list of stock photo sources to get you started, see the bibliography.) At an early age, my students learn to respect copyright restrictions. Perhaps their understanding has something to do with the pride of ownership they take in their own visual productions. Visual storytelling presents many excellent opportunities to discuss ethical and legal issues that students will continue to deal with throughout their academic careers.

Measurably Mine

The eight third graders in this literature circle were developing digital stories about dolphins. Yet the children had selected many different genres and various visual media to communicate information. Further, the students represented a range of reading levels, technical knowledge, and writing skills. How does a teacher evaluate such diverse products? Again, inspiration came from a staff development workshop, where I learned from a colleague how to work with my students and collaborate with other teachers to develop a "rubric of excellence."

For the purposes of this project, we decided to include the following requirements:

WRITING
- Our story will reflect a particular genre of literature.
- Our story will reflect research and knowledge about dolphins.
- Our story will have at least three distinct clusters of information.
- We will identify at least four words for thesaurus research, and include descriptive language.

PRODUCTION
- We will develop a story web.
- We will develop a script.
- We will develop a storyboard.
- Our images and text will correlate.
- Our digital story will contain between eight and twelve slides, including titles and credits.
- Our slide sequence will correlate to our storyboard.

COLLABORATION
- We will be able to identify the contributions of each team member.
- We will credit our sources of information.

QUALITY
- Our imagery and audio will be clear and easy to understand.
- We will use correct spelling and grammar.

Our rubrics have three benchmarks of mastery:

2 = I did a thorough job. This reflects excellence!
1 = I did a good job, but I could have done better.
NY = Not yet! I need to go back and work on this a bit more, then resubmit my work.

Figure 3.8 shows a completed rubric, with annotations. The rubric, along with the tools of story building—index cards, storyboards, story webs, source information—went into a project folder that students could access whenever they came into the media center to work.

Organization and management are important when guiding any student project. Adding a small box or line beside each point enabled the rubric to

Your name here: Josh

Peer Evaluator: Jackie

The City of Ember
Composite Photo and Prose

Directions: Compare your work with the standards that we set. Be very honest! Rate your work:

1= I did a thorough job. This reflects excellence!
2= I did a good job, but I could have done a better job in this area.
NY= Not yet! I need to go back and work on this a bit more, and re-submit my work.

Here is what you said that an excellent piece of work should contain:	Here is my evaluation of my project:	Here is a peer evaluation of my project:	Here is my teacher's evaluation of my project:
My photographs are clear.	2	1	1
My images and words reflect the same mood.	2	1	2
My image reflects the story setting.	1	1	1
The elements in my photograph are in proportion.	2	1	1
I chose the highly descriptive words in my writing.	2	2	2
My prose is written in first person.	1	1	1
The text on my image is legible.	1	1	1

Josh - You just need to power up your words a bit - be more descriptive. (THESAURUS)

Josh- You thought through this problem logically & sequentially — Try a critical friend to see if you can make your word choices richer — good job all around, though — and great visuals!

Figure 3.8 Jackie acted as Josh's peer evaluator in helping him to determine the effectiveness of his project on Jeanne Duprau's *The City of Ember*.

serve double duty as a checklist. Students marked off the project requirements as they fulfilled each one. However, I prefer that they *evaluate* each step at the completion of the project because only then can they accurately assess the parts in relationship to the whole. A team of students may have developed a storyboard, but if the storyboard does not correlate to the script and if the script does not address the plan set forth in the story web, then the requirements have not been fully met. I observed and met informally with teams as they worked through the stages to help them make any necessary connections.

It also is my job to make sure that the rubric addresses curriculum standards. For example, expository writing benchmarks for third-grade students include story-web development and the ability to craft an essay with an introduction, three paragraphs with correct transitions, and a conclusion. Our digital stories, regardless of the literary genres selected by the students, have to meet these writing standards. A clear and detailed rubric enables students to work independently and understand the purpose and process of a project. It also gives them ownership of their work because they have helped set the standards for excellence.

Every teacher has students working at different levels, and each child has distinctive skills, background knowledge, and preferred learning styles. In spite of that, we often feel pressured to march lockstep to ensure that we cover all the subjects, standards, and benchmarks. Experienced teachers quickly discover that true learning is a winding road, complete with hills, valleys, and ever-changing speed limits. At its core, learning remains a very human business and, therefore, gets messy at times. I believe there is a great deal of value in the "ahas!" that stimulate students to revisit their work, fill holes, and see connections between the various incarnations of information they produce through visual storytelling. Choosing to teach in a context that honors individual growth is, ultimately, the difference between cultivating a desire for true excellence and that deadly "what-do-I-have-to-do-to-pass" mentality. When we know our students, we find that we are able to help them pace and examine their work to achieve meaningful learning.

In the case of digital stories, I find that students are intrinsically motivated to do their best. The hard work of research, writing, and planning is rewarded by the hands-on technology, creative collaboration, and innovative communication. They produce something that is uniquely theirs. Further, students know that their peers will view their work. They want to do a good job and feel pride in the outcome. When I praised Kyle for his excellent digital project, he responded happily, "It is good! I didn't know I had it in me!"

Indeed, I often find that my greatest challenge as their guide and teacher lies in getting the students to wrap up their productions. They become so engaged in the process that they don't want it to end, and often find ways to finesse it to death in order to remain in the creative and productive

80

state of "story showing." However, because they have helped determine the standards of excellence, they are more motivated to use those goals to guide their work. Like a piece of art, no two stories will be alike. Yet each story serves, with the unique imprint of any truly creative endeavor, to demonstrate mastery of skills within various subjects, modalities, and standards.

We Have Met the Twenty-First-Century Teachers . . . And They Are Us

Up to this point in our digital storytelling project, the third graders had been layering images vertically to add depth and meaning to their images. With my help, they had also been combining text and imagery to convey meaning. Experimenting with opacity, we decided this time to integrate images horizontally, in collage form, in response to the question "How can we show the relationship between Mila and her dolphin family?" Mila slowly acquires language skills as the story progresses, but the author also conveys the character's discomfort with limiting communication to only the "human" way or the "dolphin" way. The book offers a way for students to explore the relationship of multiple forms of communication—for example, how music and imagery or body language and text work together to convey mood and messages.

I helped students prepare for this project by accessing about fifty stock photographs and storing them in a folder on the school's network drive. I experimented with digital collage techniques and demonstrated the procedures to the class. Students combined photos, varying the opacity and overlaying filters. The children offered many creative solutions. Zach added subtle text, manipulating the words to look as if they might be ripples in the ocean. Ana composed a tune, played it on her recorder, and used PowerPoint software to embed the music into her image. Brea, ever the writer, penned an original poem to strengthen and support the wistful mood of her imagery.

The students' ability to communicate visually was evident, both in their products and in their interpretation of the assignment. Clearly they were gaining proficiency in communicating big ideas, and their work was becoming increasingly abstract. They were integrating several forms of literacy to create effective and intelligent solutions to their problem-based projects. They were making independent, thoughtful choices about the presentation of ideas. Of course, they were working at varying levels of sophistication, but their projects demonstrated understanding of how the order, combination, and layering of images conveyed different meanings. As they read, wrote, researched, discussed, and created, they were learning a great deal about collaboration, critical thinking, and problem solving. Typical of today's digital natives, the students also explored new applications of technology and tended to put their discoveries to use immediately, blazing a trail that others could follow. For example, Jory figured out that he could flatten the layers of his collage images and then manipulate the saturation and hue to visually unify his collection of images. Immediately, several other students began experimenting with this technique and linked their ideas to Jory's discovery.

I had found a method for literature-centered, problem-based learning and was finding more and more ways to fit further disciplines and skills into our learning scenarios. My skill and confidence in technology applications were growing along with the students' knowledge. Community-based collaboration had eclipsed instructor-mandated "task learning." I was continuing to develop frameworks and rubrics to keep everyone organized and on task. Teaching had become very exciting.

In fact, we were all enthusiastic about what we were learning how to do. Students were teaching other students. Teachers were coming in after school to participate in workshops. Parents and their children were learning together through our new intergenerational after-school club, "The Samsula Snappers." Some students chose to give up recess time to work on their projects in the media center.

We may agree that this all sounds great. It's creative, active learning. The kids love it. Everyone participates. Everyone is motivated. It's integrative and inclusive. It's powerful stuff. But today's expectations and climate compel us to ask just how it contributes to that long list of acquired skills we must check off in the name of educational legislation. So let's examine the way that this methodology addresses those very real expectations. As school districts scramble to simultaneously address "drill-the-skill" mandates and meet twenty-first-century expectations, the philosophy of working "smarter, not harder" comes into its own. When we ask empowered teachers what they value, technology inclusion is mentioned time and time again. It is part of today's schoolscape, and it is here to stay. Technology doesn't change what we teach—the core disciplines remain the same—but it does affect how we teach and how children learn and express their understanding.

In his book *A Whole New Mind*, author Daniel Pink (2006) sets a wide framework for why, and how, we learn, tracing the evolution of the United States through the Age of Agriculture, through the Industrial Age, and into the Information Age. As our nation continues to outsource labor and increasingly relays white-collar jobs to other countries, he suggests that we are entering the "Conceptual Age," that is, a period when our economic value and worth will lie not in our ability to perform tasks, nor in specific skill knowledge, but in our ability to create and to conceptualize. He builds a compelling case as he lists and describes half a dozen creative skills essential for a thriving twenty-first-century citizen and describes the roles those creative skills will play in the working world.

If the ultimate goal of education is to prepare students to live successfully and contribute to their local and global communities, which adds up to a sizable piece of real estate, it seems rather important that we find ways to incorporate these real-life skills into our classrooms regularly. When students communicate in a visual language, they meet learning standards on many levels. Their work addresses core language arts skills, national technology standards, and critical-thinking skills. With literature and research at the core of each project, students are reading, writing, researching, speaking, and listening. They are examining and expressing themes and metaphors, investigating the writer's purpose, and analyzing plots and subplots. They are expanding their visual and verbal vocabularies. They are linking ideas to other disciplines. The breadth of problem-based learning demands that they interpret, analyze, and translate information. Higher-thinking skills of evaluation and synthesis come into play as students construct, critique, and justify their work. They prepare to contribute to the twenty-first century as they hone those real-life skills of creation, collaboration, design, and innovation.

Granted, project-based learning requires time, preparation, and analysis on the part of the instructor. It was an organically learned process for me, combining study and practice, creativity and flexibility, humility and humor. But consider the breadth and depth of content we are able to cover when we begin to think, and to teach, in terms of meaningful components of information and experience. A master plan results in a masterpiece, with everyone learning, everyone growing, everyone benefiting. We find ourselves more responsive to our students' desire for broad, interactive experiences, and our willingness to enter their world inspires them to take ownership of their own learning. Before we know it, we realize that we have advanced on the time continuum. We are twenty-first-century teachers!

Research: The Fourth R

I can't believe all the things I've figured out how to do. You make me feel so smart.—Austin, age 10

A group of fifth graders is at work in the school media center. The students are engaged in an interdisciplinary study that brings together literature, social studies, and visual art. This particular group, selected by their classroom teachers for language arts enrichment, are reading Blue Balliet's *Chasing Vermeer,* and now the students are viewing online galleries of Johannes Vermeer's work, comparing the narrative descriptions in the book with images of his paintings. Vermeer's art is infused with details about everyday life in seventeenth-century Holland. We talk about the messages conveyed through the art. Learning leaps into the creative realm when my students ask the question, "Can we make pictures like these?"

This is not an unusual request from intermediate students at our school. These students are accustomed to problem-based learning projects that integrate literature, writing, research, and technology skills. As they progress from kindergarten through fifth grade, they become increasingly adept at showing what they know in multiple formats. Based on the content of the book and the learning extensions that we have investigated, we design a project.

Always eager to get their hands on digital cameras and computers, the students definitely want to include technology applications. In earlier projects—such as a whole-class collaboration focusing on early explorers the previous semester and the electronic haiku this small group created last year—the students learned how to use filters and add text to their photos. They know how to use imaging software to create layered photos. (See Chapter 2 for more details about this process.) But the students need to master additional software skills to create images in the style of Vermeer. His realistic paintings were characterized by rich colors and dramatic use of light and shadow—classic elements of Baroque art. I make a mental note to give a whole-class demonstration of some of the advanced tools within the software program (see Can You See It? New Tools for Old Masters for more information).

CAN YOU SEE IT? NEW TOOLS FOR OLD MASTERS

Digital software programs offer a variety of tools that can transform your work into a digital representation of Rembrandt—adding richness to the color in your photo compositions, manipulating the light source for drama, and using dodge and burn tools to add mood and subtlety to your images. They can also help to unify the layers of imagery.

Some students used these tools after they combined the layers of their imagery—the background and the middle ground—but before they added their text layer. Most digital software includes saturation tools that can make the colors in your image more muted or vibrant. Adobe Photoshop Elements also has a temperature tool that enables you to adjust your work along the color spectrum, such as making your work appear cooler (blue) or warmer (magenta).

Lighting effects shine through the application of another set of filters. Use these tools to change the direction or intensity of light or to create a dramatic light source. For fine work, use the burn and dodge tools to "paint on" detailed shadow and light. Experiment with these sophisticated applications. You will amaze yourself!

As we studied the online gallery of Vermeer images, we discussed the relevance of the details in the portraits. What was Vermeer trying to tell us about the person in the painting through the clothing, the environment, and the objects included in the composition? We agree that the student-generated images should have a narrative quality—that is, they should tell a story that viewers can accurately interpret—and we decide to use both written and visual narrative devices in the project. We add responsive writing to the growing list of our project outcomes. This ensures that our visual narratives will be well connected to the state standards for reading and writing at this grade level.

Do we know enough about life in seventeenth-century Holland to create images that will be authentic to the era? We agree that we do not. This means that additional historical research will be in order. It will be my job to find material on this topic, at a reading level that is appropriate for fifth graders and in a format that is accessible for their review.

87

A research component on Holland's gilded age may seem a bit of a stretch for ten- and eleven-year-olds, but it relates directly to our literature study, links nicely with previous studies on Europe's Renaissance, and promises to provide an interesting application of the research skills they have been developing over the past several years. The proposed project also will involve collaboration, as students share and synthesize the information they glean. We decide to use "quick-fact" research (more on this method later in this chapter) to help us gather, organize, and prioritize the information we need.

As our discussion unfolds, we create an outline of needs and outcomes. My teacher to-do list starts to grow as well: I need to assemble a list of kid-friendly historical sites, access our state's Sunlink online catalog to browse and borrow additional reading material from nearby schools, and compile a folder of stock photo backgrounds to be used in the photo project. Cross-referencing curriculum standards for fifth-grade language and literacy, social studies, visual art, and technology education helps me tighten and refine this project.

This project addresses the following State Curriculum Standards, excerpted from Florida's Sunshine State Standards for grades 3–5 (State of Florida Department of Education 1996):

SOCIAL STUDIES
• Uses a variety of sources to understand history
• Understands various aspects of family life, structures, and rules in different cultures and many eras
• Knows development in the humanities

LANGUAGE ARTS
- Clarifies understanding by checking other sources and by discussion
- Prepares for writing by focusing on a central theme and identifying a purpose for writing
- Uses electronic technology to create, revise, retrieve, and verify information
- Creates a narrative in which ideas, details, and events are relevant to the story line
- Understands that word choices can shape reactions, perceptions, and beliefs
- Selects and uses appropriate technology to enhance communications

VISUAL ARTS
- Understands how artists have used visual symbols across time
- Understands perceived similarities and differences between different genres of art

The project also addresses the following standards from National Educational Technology Standards (International Society for Technology in Education 2008):

- Uses technology tools to enhance learning, increase productivity, and promote creativity
- Uses a variety of media to communicate ideas and information effectively

And it addresses these skill standards from Partnership for 21st Century Skills:

- Demonstrates originality and inventiveness in work
- Identifies and asks significant questions that clarify various points of view
- Frames, analyzes, and synthesizes information in order to solve problems and answer questions
- Articulates thoughts and ideas clearly through speaking and writing
- Assumes shared responsibility for collaborative work
- Understands how media messages are constructed, and for what purpose
- Uses technology as a tool to research, organize, and communicate

It may sound like a lot of preparation on the teacher's part, but the planning frees me to act as a guide and mentor as students work through these multiple processes during the school day. The stage is set for a rich learning experience that will enable students to integrate several subject disciplines, apply sophisticated research skills, and strengthen visual, oral, and written communication.

The initial project concepts will form the backbone of a rubric that will keep students focused and help them assess their progress. The final photographs, along with students' presentations of their work, will demonstrate mastery of technology, research, and visual literacy skills.

STEPPING BACK IN TIME

It's time to get started. The students' first job is to create a character who might have lived within the historical period and context suggested by Vermeer's work. Using online and text research, students develop pictures of citizens in every walk of life—servants, shopkeepers, shippers, adults, children, and people of both poverty and wealth. Being thrifty, we find some items from home and some leftovers from our school Renaissance festival and assemble a community table of props and costumes to stimulate our thinking. Once again referencing the online photo gallery, the fifth graders work together to develop and refine their photo compositions.

"Let's have more than one person in our photo," suggests ten-year-old Jewell. I think it would be a good idea to show a lady and a servant together so that people could compare them."

She enlists the help of her classmate, Adriana, to play the role of the lady's servant, which expands the original concept. In another section of the media center, some students set the stage for their portrait shoot before they start snapping digital shots.

Meanwhile, Alex, Rebecca, and Jesse, who have already finished their portrait shoot, work at the computer station. Browsing through the folder of stock photo backgrounds located on the school's student network storage drive, they use computer software to merge their photos with the visual representation of themes and ideas they chose for their portraits.

"I want my writing paper to look like parchment," explains Rebecca. She uses new software-imaging skills to shade a document she included in her composition to indicate that her subject was a literate person. "And I have to figure out how to make the picture show light and shadow like Vermeer did. I'm going to look at the [photo] gallery again to get some ideas."

Another student who is new to our school is having trouble merging his images and calls out for help. "Well, I'm stuck!" he says with frustration. I walk over to help him, and another student leans over my shoulder for a quick consultation. The more experienced classmate quickly realizes that the struggling student has accidentally "locked" the layers of the photo application tools (see Can You See It? Merging and Locking Layers). I listen as he patiently coaches his friend out of the dilemma, teaching him how to use the toolbar to add or delete text and special effects.

CAN YOU SEE IT? MERGING AND LOCKING LAYERS

Remember those clear report covers? Imagine that you have drawn a simple image on several of those transparent pages. What happens when you stack them together? Of course, you will see all of the images. That's exactly the way that Adobe Photoshop Elements works. Each layer stacks on top of the other. You can rearrange the layers, delete layers that you no longer want, change the opacity of a layer, and add filter and text layers. This is where building imagery really becomes fun!

A navigation bar on the side lets you see each layer. The bottom layer, that is, the background layer, is always locked. This keeps that layer in one place. Once in a while, students (and teachers, too) accidentally lock additional layers, making it impossible for them to edit or merge the layers. If this happens, the mistake is easy to fix. All you have to do is look at your layer bar, find the layer you are having trouble with, and check to see if there is a "lock" icon beside that layer. Unlocking a layer is as simple as a click of the mouse. Just position your cursor over the lock icon, give it a click, and you are back in business.

In another area, a cluster of students is involved in an impromptu writer's workshop that includes communicating through text and imag-

I write in an old book a secret not to be told.
I have dreams of my own—to become a painter, and to
travel to unexplored places. Let open the gates and fly free.
Though I hope, it will not happen. [...] *women are kept at home.*
[...] *will keep striving.*
[...] *ill never surrender.*
[...] *ay, I will fly free.*

Miranda, age 10

Figure 4.1 Miranda's portrait and text overlay.

ery. Building on their research of life in seventeenth-century Holland, the students are collaborating and coaching each other through a first-person narrative of their imaginary lives as citizens of Delft. They began using thesaurus skills regularly during the previous school year, and they continue to access this tool to choose the strongest, most descriptive words as they develop word pictures of life in historic Holland.

Miranda uses her research about women of that era to develop the character of a shipper's daughter. She explains her accompanying photograph. "I live in a wealthy house," Miranda says, "but that doesn't mean that my life is perfect. I am not allowed to do the things my brothers can do. I want to go on a trader's ship and make drawings and maps of the things there, but I have to stay at home."

Her explanation indicates her understanding of the role of women in Dutch society, of Holland's participation in global shipping, and of emerging cartography skills. Satisfied with her final written draft, Miranda moves back to the computer to add this text overlay to her self-portrait (see Figure 4.1).

Meanwhile, Melissa reads her narrative aloud to the group. "You need an ending," one student suggests after Melissa finishes. Another classmate compliments Melissa on her sentence describing the fatigue her character feels while attending to the endless duties of a large household (see Figure 4.2).

Alex is new to our school and is just learning how to work with a thesaurus to expand his vocabulary choices. I spend some time showing him how to use the thesaurus, including how to decide when to use simple language and when to select more sophisticated words. "I like the sound of *opulent*," he decides, discarding the word *rich* in favor of this more descriptive choice.

Ordinary People, Extraordinary Times

The skills and processes described in the Vermeer project, and the various forms of communication that go along with it, are prime examples of the range of technology-driven competencies that define today's literacy. A closer look at the students' work reveals the rich integration of imagery and text. Students are thoughtfully incorporating selected symbols. They are gathering and interpreting information about the cultural and social framework of Vermeer's life in many formats—through text, time lines, visual representations, and audio links. And they are collaborating as a learning community. As students flow through these processes, their roles shift from independent learners, to group collaborators, to shared problem solvers and, finally, to creative communicators. All of these processes ultimately synthesize in a meaningful product that demonstrates a student's newly acquired knowledge and skills.

Creative technology applications are powerful motivators for students of every learning style. Research shows that students remember more when they are engaged in multimodal learning (Metiri Group/Cisco 2008). It remains a very real and persistent part of their world. I have never had a

I am worried
and fatigued.
A widow,
with few resources
to run my household.
I wait in fear
for the bird beaked
physician to arrive,
for my only child
is ill downstairs
with the smallpox.
I have no
family alliance.
If I lose my child,
I will be truly alone.

Figure 4.2 This writing shows Rebecca's research on medical practices and serious illnesses of the seventeenth century. She also communicates understanding about the role of women and family structure. If you take a close look at her writing paper, you will notice that she used a dodging tool to create the look of parchment.

student choose *not* to take digital photographs, for example, or decline an opportunity to create projects with imaging software. New and attractive tools of communication can enhance interdisciplinary learning. The vast majority of students are willing to persist with assignments just to get to the "fun stuff" of creating and communicating through technology.

The fact is, a great deal of hard work precedes the visual literacy projects I have described. Partnered with literature and language arts, working within specific disciplines, there lies an important research component—the ability to locate, select, organize, evaluate, and apply information. This process requires students to draw on appropriate resources; read widely; write, edit, and revise; compare and connect; and present information accurately and distinctively. On the information highway, it is where the rubber meets the road.

WHAT IS RESEARCH, ANYWAY?

Does research involve fact-finding? Yes. Must students access multiple sources of information to engage in research? Absolutely. But the location, selection, and recitation of information, sometimes inelegantly referred to as "read and regurgitate" in educational circles, does not pass muster as true research. At its core, research is a creative process, requiring students to *think*. The process should be both rigorous and routine, drawing on key concepts from the core curriculum throughout the school year while continually raising the bar for students as they learn how to support and express their ideas.

The National Forum on Information Literacy was formed by the American Library Association in 1989 in response to the dramatic rise in the accessibility of what the organization deemed a "tidal wave of information"—and the accompanying challenges and logistics of using research wisely. (You can learn more about the work of the National Forum on Information Literacy at http://www.infolit.org/.) The forum provides an excellent framework for defining and teaching authentic research skills, specifically, helping learners to:

- Recognize the need for information
- Locate, choose, and organize information from a range of sources
- Create an original response
- Share the information with others

Thorough research requires sustained effort and discrimination on the part of the student. Further, it asks students to challenge their assumptions as new, better, or contradictory information comes to light. As you guide students through the research process (see Can You See It? Info-Savvy Learners—Square One), you will discover that some students will be more adept at critical thinking and creative applications, while others will struggle to connect the topic to the questions and the questions to the answers. Although some students will speed down the road of research—and I have found they are not always the most academically able students, but often those with strong analytical leanings—others will come to a screeching halt and wait for someone, anyone, to complete the journey for them. These are the students who ask that dreaded question, "Is *this* good enough?" Or, perhaps detoured along the path, they become intimidated by the task of putting so many processes together in a meaningful and creative way.

CAN YOU SEE IT? INFO-SAVVY LEARNERS—SQUARE ONE

If I had to pull just one rabbit out of the hat of the aggregate learning described in these pages, I think I would have to choose information literacy skills. These skills weave their way through every facet of visual and traditional literacy. We know that the world of information will only continue to expand. Many teachers today find themselves walking the narrow tightrope of protecting their students (Internet sources aren't rated) and providing some guidance for a door that is wide open to these kids outside of their school day. Most school districts embed firewalls into their network to narrow the range of information that students can access during school hours, and parental controls provide a safety gate for home computers. Nonetheless, we must teach our students how to find their way to the right information and how to evaluate and apply that information. Fear is not an option here. So, where do we start?

Kathy Schrock offers some parameters and excellent evaluative tools on her Discovery School site (http://school.discoveryeducation.com/schrockguide/eval.html). The authors of the Big6, Michael Eisenberg and Robert Berkowitz, have developed a junior version, the Super3, to help our youngest learners get a jump-start on locating, interpreting, and synthesizing information (http://www.big6.com/kids/K-2.htm). Something that has helped me is to strategically place the computers so that I can see each screen from one spot. I also require students to keep an Internet journal of the sites they visit. It's excellent practice for citing sources—and it keeps them accountable for their time and use of the computer.

The good news is that educational research suggests that critical-thinking skills can be taught, and that students' ability to analyze and synthesize will improve with practice. Acquiring and applying these skills takes time and, like so much else in the educational forum, is developmental. From beginning to end, a well-designed research project requires learners to offer their very best effort. That challenge alone is guaranteed to jettison some students out of their comfort zones. Be prepared for some resistance!

Consider the experiences of Jared, a reluctant reader who was progressing slowly through his independent research project about the history of football. He had a text source appropriate for his reading level but was unable to find age-appropriate information on the Internet. He wasn't really sure how to evaluate the sources, so he spent a great deal of time trying to read passages that were either too difficult or irrelevant, or both. Then he tried to rely solely on his text source, but because the book also included a substantial amount of information about the rules of the game, Jared kept losing sight of the focus of his research. He became very frustrated, unable to redirect or move forward on his own.

Helping Jared formulate a series of subtopics about the history of football and organize facts under those subtopics got him focused and moving forward. Pairing him with a "critical friend" who shared Jared's interest in football encouraged Jared to develop a broader perspective about his topic. Reading his work out loud and discussing it with a peer helped him evaluate the relevance of the facts he had gathered and develop a feeling for the way the research fit together. As Jared organized and reread his research, his friend Justin would suggest subtopics or ask questions that caused Jared to discover and plug a few gaps. Finally, selecting an alternate source of information—in this case, substituting an interview with our physical education coach for the initial Internet research—provided motivation and a student-friendly source for Jared's research. Once Jared had gathered a sufficient number of relevant facts, he picked up steam, and was able to synthesize and present his research confidently.

Breaking research projects into manageable chunks, modeling effective strategies, developing creative and authentic applications of research, and teaching students to reflect on their learning will help them become skillful navigators on the information highway.

Just the Facts, Ma'am

While today's learners have information at their fingertips, available in various languages, reading levels, and degrees of accuracy, they have to figure out what to do with the data. They must learn how to sift through a mountain of facts, evaluate and select sources, and apply them in ways that reflect their understanding of a subject or idea. This idea comes home to us when we realize that few ten-year-olds can describe Albert Einstein beyond "that scientist guy with all the crazy hair," or that a mere handful of third graders understand the historical significance of the Fourth of July holiday. So the greater question becomes: Do they know how to find out why Einstein is valued or how to research the origins of America's Independence Day? In other words, can they use the tools at hand to access and use information intelligently?

The essential research question therefore shifts from where can I find information to where can I find the *best* information? Addressing the issue of quality is far more difficult than locating a source. There is so much data out there, most of it uncensored, some of it unreliable. Students need systematic instruction and guided practice finding, evaluating, and using research.

The Chicken or the Egg?

Research begins with questions, and those questions are often borne of newly acquired information. Students learn something new and want to know more. They begin to make connections to prior knowledge. As they formulate and investigate their questions, they pick up further incidental information—interesting facts and compelling ideas. Those findings, in turn, generate further questions. Many great philosophers, writers, and scientists have found themselves lost in that rich labyrinth of possibilities, eventually burdened with so many nuances of thought that they could barely navigate their way back to the original question. Our students find themselves in good company as they take on the challenge of research.

Structural models, such as Michael Eisenberg and Robert Berkowitz's Big6 model (http://www.big6.com/kids/), keep students focused, and help them organize, prioritize, and sift through information and ideas. The Big6 model is presented in developmentally appropriate formats, allow-ing primary students to grasp basic research skills and then to broaden and deepen those skills as they gain knowledge and maturity.

Research models can also act as evaluative tools; for example, the K–W–L model, developed by Donna Ogle (1986), asks students to evaluate their existing base of knowledge on a given subject, to formulate a series of questions for further investigation, and to describe what they learned as a result of independent research and active reading. Corresponding questions help students measure their progress in reaching the goals of research. Visual, graphical, and writing processes assist students in the synthesis and presentation of the information they collect.

Children are naturally curious. Questions and theories arise as they read stories, study science and history, experience life, and search for their place in the world. We can build on that fresh joy as we help them respond to their questions. Through thoughtful instruction and assessment, we can model and teach sound research skills to students of all ages.

LOOSENING THE REINS

In the spirit of empowering students for lifelong learning, we want to bring them to the place where they are able to use research, writing, and reporting skills for their own purposes. What happens when they are asked to gather information for independent research?

I have abridged a range of research models to develop a four-question sequence that guides my students through these stages of research:

- What do I want to know? (Devising a research topic and questions)
- Where do I need to go? (Identifying sources for research)
- What do I now know? (Gathering and organizing information)
- How will I show what I know? (Sharing findings)

Organized as headings on a checklist, which students keep in their research folders along with their findings, these questions keep them focused and moving forward.

The very first thing that students will need to do is devise a topic for their research. The next step is to ascertain whether appropriate informational sources are available. ("Appropriate," in this sense, means appropriate to the students' grade and/or reading level.) I remind students that their research can only be as good as the sources they access. The library's electronic catalog is a good first stop for those resources. Students unable to find the right materials within our collection access our interlibrary loan system to find out whether the materials they need are available from other schools within our district. (Requiring at least one school-based resource goes a long way toward helping students select appropriate topics; many suggested independent studies on Freddie Krueger or *Halo* have died on the vine in light of this stipulation.)

When they are confident they can find the resources they need, students are ready to address step one in depth, devising a set of questions that pertain to their topic. Formulating specific questions fine-tunes the range of information that students are seeking and helps them to identify appropriate secondary sources. Through these initial processes working symbiotically, we address two basic areas of research: what do I want to know, and where do I need to go (to find information)?

Many students, no matter how many times they have engaged in guided research projects, will struggle with their first attempts to conduct independent research. For example, Brittany became frustrated when she was unable to find the answers to her questions in an independent study of gardening. A closer look at her questions revealed that she was actually searching for information, not about gardens, but about seeds. Fine-tuning the topic to match her areas of inquiry helped her locate the information she needed. William tapped into a wealth of resources about basketball but then realized that the facts he gathered, while related to his topic, did not address any of his questions. He was so excited to make the connection between the questions and the research that he came into the media center on his own time to rework his project.

Some students will get so immersed in the process of gathering information that they can't seem to make the transition to the next phase of summarizing and synthesizing data. Others will struggle to identify the most basic of facts and put these ideas on paper. Some students, who are great critical and creative thinkers are less adept at reading and need to be supported in finding, analyzing, and applying information in alternate formats.

Knowing our students' strengths and weaknesses and recognizing the fluid nature of their skills, depending on the topic and context, is critical if we want to make information relevant and accessible to all. Alternate sources of information, CD-ROMS, videos, books on tape, and the highly visual DK Eyewitness Books series (Dorling Kindersley) are some of the additional sources students can use to explore research topics with increasing independence. And don't overlook your personal resources and connections. One of my students, Timothy, wanted to learn more about submarines. I put him in touch with a naval submarine officer (my brother Jay) for a telephone interview on the subject. Another expert from the nearby University of Florida graciously agreed to be interviewed by a fourth grader on the topic of Little Big Horn. This telephone conversation provided rich material for Hunter's delightfully fresh slant on a social studies project entitled "Was General Custer a Good Listener?" (Hunter's conclusion: he was not.)

A cut-and-paste strategy for organizing research addresses our third question—what do I now know?—by helping students put their findings together and credit their sources. The students use "quick-fact" research pages (see Figures 4.3 and 4.4). The top of each page provides a space to credit the source of information. Below are five sections that students use to record the facts that they gather as they research. Students use one quick-fact page for each information source they access. Each fact section is divided by a dotted line, which the students use to cut their sheets into separate sections. Now they must further analyze the information they have gathered as they physically organize it. The most relevant facts take prominence, with those that seem to support or add additional details beneath. Sometimes students will find during this process that they have replicated facts. Occasionally, they will realize that they have gathered conflicting information from their sources and will go scurrying back to verify their findings and make decisions about the accuracy of their research sources. Sometimes they may see that, while they have a great deal of detailed information about one aspect of their topic, they have barely touched on, or perhaps neglected altogether, other important aspects of their research topic.

Investigation Page_____

Source #2 Internet

Please write the address

here:_____

Please use full sentences to list facts:

_____

Fact

#1:_____

_____

_____

Fact#2:_____

_____

_____

Fact#3:_____

_____

_____

Fact#4:_____

_____

_____

Fact#5:_____

_____

_____

_____

Figure 4.3   A sample quick-fact sheet for Internet sources.

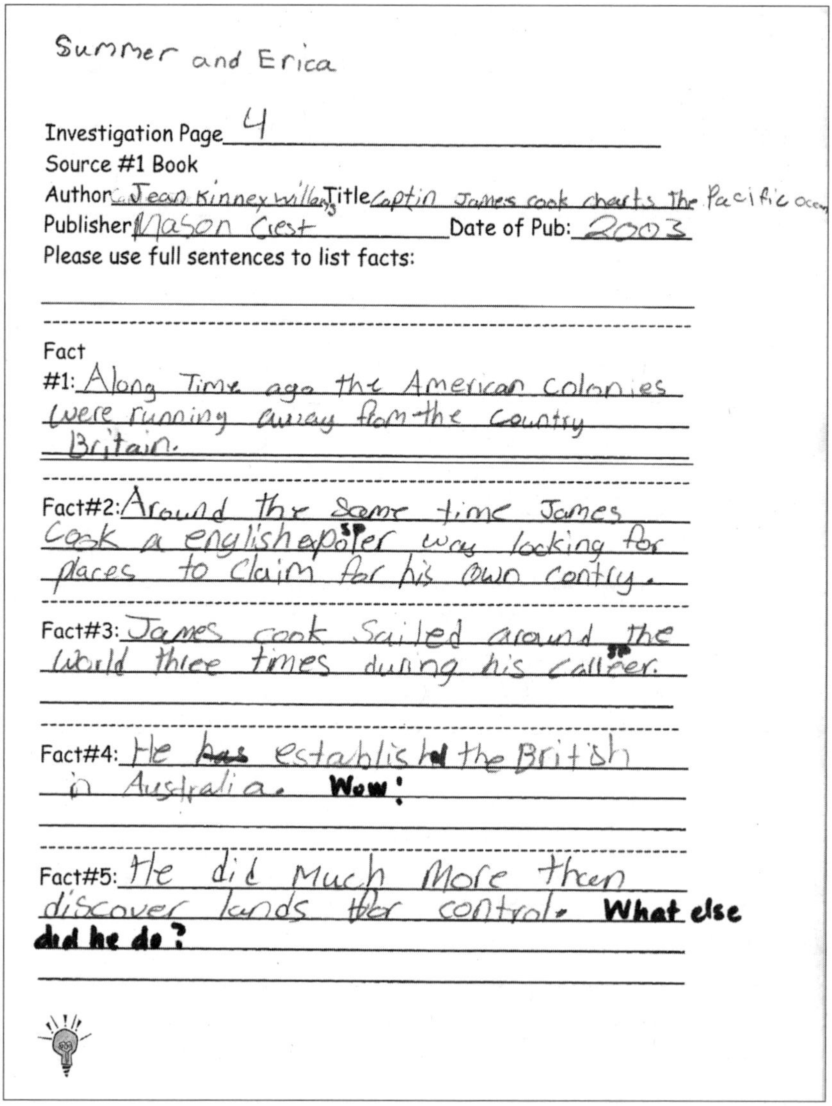

Summer and Erica

Investigation Page _4_

Source #1 Book

Author: _Jean Kinney Williams_ Title _Captin James Cook charts the Pacific ocean_

Publisher _Mason Crest_   Date of Pub: _2003_

Please use full sentences to list facts:

Fact
#1: _A long Time ago the American colonies were running away from the country Britain._

Fact#2: _Around the same time James Cook a english explorer was looking for places to claim for his own contry._

Fact#3: _James cook Sailed around the world three times during his callrer._

Fact#4: _He has established the British in Australia._ **Wow!**

Fact#5: _He did Much More then discover lands ther control._ **What else did he do?**

Figure 4.4 A completed quick-fact sheet. This enthusiastic research team used two book sources and two Internet sources to gather information about Captain James Cook.

This process nearly always leads to adjustment on the students' part. They will often go back to their sources or access additional sources to round out their findings. A "critical friend" comes in handy here, someone who can help young researchers craft a body of knowledge by asking questions and

Figure 4.5 These fifth graders are engaged in various stages of the research process—gathering, evaluating, and organizing information.

seeking clarification of the facts that have been assembled. In addition, this is an excellent juncture for the classroom teacher to examine the students' efforts and provide formal feedback and guidance.

After the students have organized their facts and have made their additions or clarifications, they can use a glue stick to affix their work to a legal-sized sheet of paper. The sources of information are placed below the facts. Younger students can follow the same format. Working in research teams, each child provides one source of information and records his or her findings on a simple, three-line quick-fact page. Team members then work together to organize and evaluate their findings on large, chart-sized graphic organizers. Physically analyzing their research in this way shows students how to arrange their information for maximum impact (see Figure 4.5).

As they mature and get more practice organizing research, students become more confident and sophisticated in their choices. For example, Courtney's topic "The Life of Harriet Tubman" suggested a chronological order because the research was biographical. Courtney organized her find-ings sequentially, beginning with Harriet Tubman's childhood as a slave in Maryland and concluding with Tubman's participation in the women's suffrage movement. By contrast, Cassia organized her work in "chunks"—identifying connections, and then putting components of related infor-mation together. Her research on dogs that work with humans followed a general introduction with subheadings for police and rescue dogs, guide dogs, and hunting dogs. Each of these girls followed a similar system for accessing and evaluating information. But they chose different organiza-tional forms to link their information together in a way that best fit their respective topics. Organizing research findings in a way that makes sense requires thoughtful decision making.

Graphic organizers or software, such as Inspiration or Kidspiration, draw on students' visual literacy skills to provide a framework for assem-bling information, helping them make the leap from collecting loosely related facts to synthesizing a body of knowledge. (The Lee's Summit, Missouri, R–7 School District provides links to a wide selection of graphic organizers, along with ideas and examples for using them. See http://its. leesummit.k12.mo.us/graphic_organizers.htm for more information.) As teachers, we also can model the skills of organizing and synthesizing infor-mation, demonstrating how research, writing, and visual imagery can be used to communicate throughout our lives.

BRICK BY BRICK

Most students today respond to the word *research* by heading directly to the computer. I have to admit that I am first in line to preach the wonders of the Internet. Thoughtful searches through this portal can reveal millions of authentic sources at the click of the mouse.

Yet Internet tracking is just one method of gathering information, and the resources available through computer culling are not limitless. Rigor-ous research involves finding, evaluating, synthesizing, and applying infor-mation, not just looking up a topic on World Book Online and pressing the print button. Authentic inquiry should include a broad range of resources

and multiple methods of locating them. For example, while students typically know about print and Internet resources, do they also know how to
find and evaluate audio and video sources such as movies, television shows,
and books on tape? Are they familiar with sources including original documents, interviews, and personal experiences? Can they make use of inferential sources, such as information gathered from literature? There is a
valuable place for each of those resources in the investigative process. Effective research employs a variety of perspectives and formats. As teachers, our
task is to guide students through the field and show them how to choose
and synthesize resources into a unified and purposeful presentation.

Consider the following research activity that tied into the third-grade
social studies curriculum and enabled students to explore ancient Egypt
using contemporary tools. We narrowed our topic to "King Tut" for the
purpose of practicing multiple-source research skills. Using a large paper
triangle, sticky notes, and pencils, we worked as a class to build a "pyramid
of knowledge" using several formats. A small class set of *Tut's Mummy:
Lost . . . and Found* by Judy Donnelly, written at a third-grade reading
level, was a friendly source for independent reading. A *Reading Rainbow*
video segment filmed in the antiquities section of the Boston Museum of
Fine Arts provided an appropriate second source. Internet sources, which
I preselected and organized in a folder under "Favorites," acted as a third
source of information.

I chose a range of Internet sources, below, on, and above the third-grade
reading level. I looked for sources with a rich balance of visual and textual
information and easy-to-follow links. I also searched for a few links with
audio and video components so that my struggling readers would be able
to gather information efficiently. I wanted to create a way to gather and
organize information that would engage auditory, visual, and kinesthetic
learners. As students rotated through the information stations during
the course of their lesson, they were asked to find three quick facts about
King Tut and to write each of those facts in sentence form on a sticky note.
The rectangular sticky notes, further organized by subtopic as a concluding activity, would form the bricks of our pyramid of knowledge. Students
used the information in a subsequent collaboration to develop summary
paragraphs of the findings.

This process sounds straightforward, and for many students, multiple resource exercises such as this one are easy to do. In its *Information Literacy Standards for Student Learning* (1998), the American Library Association asks students to consider whether "the information gathered is well fitted to the informational needs." I paraphrase this objective in simpler terms, asking my students if the "answer matches the question." This inquiry has been met with many a furrowed brow as students grapple with the idea that research should lead to a particular outcome—not just locating a fact, but locating information that is directly relevant to the topic investigated or questions asked. I encounter students at every age and every stage of the research process who have difficulty connecting the fact with the topic, the question with the answer. In this particular exercise, Nate wrote, "Lord Carnavan was losing hope after five years of digging." It is a fact that relates to the discovery of Tut's tomb, but Nate was unable to make that connection. In fact, he was not really sure what he had written. He had faithfully copied words from a source (they sounded important) but did not fully understand what he had read.

This provided an opportunity for one-on-one coaching about the relevancy of research, but I also could have designed a mini-lesson to reinforce this point for a small or large group of students who were similarly confused. One of the most important considerations is making sure that the information is on the child's reading level. The text on many websites is written for an audience beyond the age of eight. In Nate's case, we went back to the source (National Geographic Kids online, one of the sites I selected for our "Favorites" folder) together, found the context for that statement, read a bit further, and linked the information directly to the topic by adding the phrase, "and searching for King Tut's tomb."

Students at the beginning of the research process must be gently and constantly reminded that they need to understand information before they can share it effectively with others. As we gather and note research, we ask ourselves two questions: Do I understand what I just wrote? If the answer is yes, we move on to the second question: Can I organize/phrase/share this information in a way that everyone can understand? This process is modeled many times in the primary grades as we synthesize the information gathered into narrative form. Eventually, the process of research for the purpose of real learning becomes clearer to the students.

For example, the first-grade teachers and I took advantage of a science curriculum study on spiders to model the processes of acquiring, organizing, and applying information. Each first grader was provided with a Spider Science notebook, a collection of index cards in which holes have been punched along the left-hand side. Rubber bands are threaded through the holes and held in place by a tongue depressor "spine." (This form of binding makes it easy for students to take their pages apart and physically organize and edit the information they gather.) As we read through a range of genres of literature on spiders, students learned that factual information was imbedded into many forms of literature. A thorough discussion of fiction and nonfiction literature was woven through the research as students added to their notebooks. (Interestingly, their information was notated both in text and in visual forms.) We synthesized the students' facts and developed a web-shaped graphic system, organizing common information and developing subtopics such as what spiders look like, what spiders eat, and so on. As a culminating activity, these young researchers translated their collection of information into colorful drawings of spiders, with supporting visual details to provide context about the habits and habitats of particular spiders (the type of webs woven, the preferred diet, the surrounding environment, the challenge of predators), matching their drawings to text. Technological skills came into play as students scanned their images and linked textual and visual information with Microsoft Power-Point software. The resulting work was linked together into an electronic book.

WORKING SMARTER. AGAIN.

As mentioned earlier, part of my daily work in the media center involves facilitating literature circles for our third-, fourth-, and fifth-grade students. The students are recommended for these small-group classes by their classroom teacher. Some students rotate in and out for short periods during the school year; others participate throughout the year, depending on their particular learning needs and interests. With a work of literature at the foundation, we engage in integrated instruction—reading, writing, theorizing, investigating, and applying technology. I often will select a book that correlates with grade-level science and social studies as a way to bolster student learning in these subject areas. Let's take a look at the role that research skills play in an integrated learning environment.

One fifth-grade unit centered on Christopher Paul Curtis's book *Bud, Not Buddy,* a work of historical fiction. With skill and love, Curtis manages to impart a view of life in the 1930s through the eyes of Bud, a high-spirited ten-year-old, who tends to surmount every obstacle through his foundation of values, resourcefulness, and humor.

I wanted my students to research the American Depression era but had difficulty finding a range of age-appropriate resources for research on this particular subject. Then it occurred to me that this topic might be just the one to teach primary sources and to practice interview skills. Every student in the group had some family friend or relative who had lived during the Depression. It was an eye-opening connection for these ten-year-olds who, I discovered, rarely view historical events in relation to the real lives of the people around them, and even more rarely connect those to their own lives. As the students shared stories and discussed their interviews, it was clear that a new vocabulary list was forming. Words like *bread line, hobo, Dust Bowl, truck farming,* and *Hooverville* emerged. We used that vocabulary list as the basis for our next level of research.

In looking at Internet sources, students came across the compelling photographs of Margaret Bourke-White. The fifth graders were electrified by the power of these images, connecting them with their interviews and discussions, and immediately asked if they could make "pictures like these." Working within the definition of historical fiction, weaving the stories of actual events through the lives of fictional characters, the students began to gather information about the Depression era and to blend it with original stories. The added challenge of writing in an acrostic format, using the letters of names of their characters as the first letter of each line of their narratives, made the phrasing a bit more poetic and the vocabulary richer.

Because we also had been talking about point of view, we made this a team activity, with each of two characters describing the same events through their particular perspectives. For example, David and Kyle developed a powerful, direct story of two brothers who leave their failing family farm in hope of finding work in a large industrial city (see Figure 4.6).

Figure 4.6 David and Kyle make revisions to their story of two brothers, Billy and Johnny Lee. In their story, Billy hops a train to get to the city and find work. In his travels, Billy meets hobos, experiences a Hooverville, and tries to evade the railroad security guards. Johnny Lee remains on the family farm and tries to keep things running while dealing with the steady stream of people who pass the farm looking for food or work.

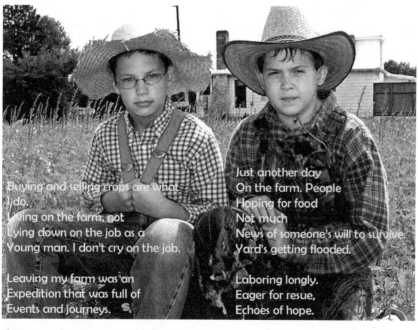

Figure 4.7 Acrostic writing format abridges and dramatizes the boys' tale in their finished product.

Samantha and Shelby devised a narrative about a desperate mother and child trapped in a rural setting without resources. Jillian and Kayla wrote a story about two sisters whose relatives were unwilling to take them in after the loss of their parents. The students then assumed the roles of the characters they created, staging and taking photographs to illustrate and support the stories they had developed. Imaging software enabled them to recreate the look of period photographs and to layer their stories over their images (see Figure 4.7 for David and Kyle's finished product).

These tales were unfailingly dramatic. But they evidenced real empathy, too. The stories, inspired by their interviews with people close to the students and strengthened by their original images, clearly echoed the desperation and courage of many Americans during this period in our history. The unfolding of events within the student narratives—the Dust Bowl, separation of families, and the dangers inherent in train hopping—gave evidence to their research on this period in America's history.

AUTHENTIC LEARNING

A natural response to inquiry, research lies at the heart of authentic learning. As teachers, we cultivate research skills as a way to empower our students to become lifelong learners. The world is at their fingertips, just waiting to be discovered. We can unlock that world for them. Purposefully linked with curriculum, research and higher-thinking skills not only address but power up a myriad of benchmarks and standards. Student research is transformed into creative, applicable, and transferable knowledge when matched with writing, literature, visual literacy, real-life experiences, and technology applications. Guided practice with these components ultimately prepares students for true, independent learning and thinking. And isn't that, really, where teaching and learning begin to matter?

Research Revealed:
The Production Stage

Some kids, if they're not having fun learning, they pretty much quit
trying to learn. —Angel, age 10

It's 1958. A class of fourth graders has been learning about the Declaration of Independence. Each student has been assigned a particular Founding Father to research and write about. Using the resources on hand, the students duly write their reports. One by one, day after day, students rise and mumble a recitation of facts without ever lifting their eyes from their papers. The rest of the students spend their time daydreaming, staring out the window, and surreptitiously passing notes. A fly drones. Somewhere in the distance, a dog barks.

It's 2008. A class of fourth graders has been learning about the Declaration of Independence. Each student has been assigned a particular Founding Father to research and write about. What has changed over the course of a half century? Sadly, in some schools, only the sounds of the droning fly and the barking dog—thanks to the modern luxury of central air conditioning.

Remember the third tenet of research established by the National Forum on Informational Literacy? It asks researchers to *create an original response*. And that relates directly to the question: how will I show what I know?

It is true that the students' work is original in so much as students have summarized, and not plagiarized, the information they collected. That skill of summarizing is modeled, and reinforced, again and again as we lead students of all ages through the research process. As they draw together information from various sources into a whole, they are definitely engaged in the critical-thinking processes of analysis, evaluation, and synthesis.

How can we infuse creative-thinking skills with student research while building traditional and visual literacy skills? In other words, how can we bring what my colleague Colleen Stemple called "rigorous academics and rigorous creativity" to life? And why should we bother to do so?

It all comes back to those higher-thinking skills. Creativity is essentially a problem-solving skill. The outcome of creative problem solving is an original solution. Is it an art? Yes, in the sense that creativity generates many possible outcomes rather than a single "right answer." Can it be learned? Of course. The more we apply creative thinking to learning and life, the more proficient we become at using the skill. More good news: Everyone is creative, though some of us have more innate ability than others, just as some people are naturally musical or athletic. If you have ever used a paper clip as a multipurpose tool or found a way to reach the entire spectrum of learners in your classroom, you are creative!

The twenty-first century is calling for unprecedented contributions of creative endeavor. As teachers we are cultivating the most important crop in the world—we are in the business of growing the brains that will find innovative solutions for global challenges ahead.

You may agree in theory, but wonder how to squeeze one more requirement into your crowded day. Let's see how we can infuse creative skills into our learning culture.

AGGREGATE LEARNING: LAYERING THE SKILLS

Writing is a valuable tool for integrating creativity into the reporting process. It also helps students work around the temptation to take the easy way out by borrowing someone else's words. Creative writing also increases vocabulary, hones language skills, and sharpens critical thinking. Pairing creative writing with research and reporting can provide extra interest and challenge.

Including visual communication in the presentation of information provides another avenue for sharing knowledge and skills. Incorporating digital imagery and imaging software draws in visual learners and encourages students to communicate in more than one format. By employing these

Figure 5.1   Samantha, Kayla, and Jillian assemble costumes for their historical project.

tools, students also learn how to analyze the messages they see and hear every day in the media-saturated world. Writing, coupled with a visual component, serves as a powerful demonstration of learning. Technology plays many important roles in the new-age research and production process, whether students access the electronic card catalog, use the Internet for guided and independent research, or apply imaging software as they integrate data in creative and unexpected formats.

Research about the original thirteen colonies was paired with persuasive writing when fifth graders wove their research into a sixty-second script. After direct instruction about videotaping, students formed small groups to conduct historical research and collaborated as they created a commercial representative of their particular colony, complete with period costumes (see Figure 5.1). Results ranged from the Pennsylvania contingents' spirited musical number, "Calling All Quakers"; to catchy phrases ("New land, new hope . . . New Hampshire!"); to hard-sell infomercials that rival anything seen on televised shopping networks.

Figure 5.2 Ali transferred the skills she used in the Anna Casey project to an original poem based on *Bridge to Terabithia* by Katherine Paterson.

Fourth-grade students combined technology and research to create a series of three-dimensional books based on *Anna Casey's Place in the World* by Adrian Fogelin (see Figure 5.2 for an example). This process required creative problem solving in the form of sculptural thinking and design, as well as writing, digital imaging, technology, and research skills. The students who excel at this product form—and need opportunities to use it in school—include kinesthetic learners, conceptual thinkers, and those who see the world in multiple dimensions.

Often we will put research skills into practice by having each student in the class research some aspect of a topic. We begin by creating a list under the heading "What do you want to know about _____?" and use those questions as the basis for research. For instance, we investigated the Holocaust during our literature study of *Number the Stars* by Lois Lowry. Each student selected one question from the list (not necessarily their own). Students incorporated the results of their research, along with a stock photo visual, into a PowerPoint slide. I simply linked the slides together to create a show on the topic of the Holocaust. The result of this shared learning provided an important foundation for understanding the context of the book.

Once students experience the range of possibilities to show what they know, they begin to pick and choose their outcomes or to combine processes to create entirely new outcomes. They often confer with classmates as they work out this fourth step of the research process. I encourage the collaborative process in any creative endeavor, believing that these impromptu creator's workshops help everyone move forward and grow stronger in their communicative skills. It also cultivates a climate of sharing and acceptance, of realizing that we are all in this together as students present what they've learned.

What about those daydreaming, window-watching, note-passing recipients of their classmates' research efforts? Multimodal presentation and shared learning minimizes that final frontier of active listening quite a bit. Research shows that students who use well-designed combinations of visuals and text learn more than students who use only text. In fact, a recent study on multimodal learning through media suggests increases in learning of between 20 and 32 percent (Metiri Group/Cisco 2008).

I keep all students engaged by asking them to compose a critical-thinking question as they listen to each presentation. At the end of each demonstration, the presenter invites some of these questions, and the dialogue is especially valuable as a self-evaluation tool because students are asked to think about why they made certain choices (see Figures 5.3 and 5.4). And, of course, they revel in compliments from their peers—an effective motivator for students to put their best effort into their work.

Figure 5.3 Jackie shares her project with a group of classmates and answers questions about her work and process.

Figure 5.4 Brandon, a second-grade student, fields questions about his digital story project and the research that went into it.

WHEN TWO HEADS ARE BETTER THAN ONE

Because my work in the media center includes literature circles for students in intermediate grades, much of the convergent learning begins with literature. I often select books that correlate with grade-level standards in social studies. But classroom teachers also come to me with requests and needs centered on the state curriculum, benchmarks and standards, or teacher's editions of state adopted textbooks. Classroom and media collaborations, based on grade-level learning objectives and segued with literacy and technology goals, yield some rich, creative, and sometimes unexpected experiences for both teachers and students.

In conjunction with an earth science unit, for example, a fourth-grade teacher asked me to help her design a research project that would include identifying a rock or mineral within specific parameters and recording data such as weight, size, and classification. She also wanted to include hands-on experiments that would give students experience with Mohs hardness scale for rocks and minerals. Because we live in Florida, formerly known as "the ocean floor," the teacher required students to perform a vinegar test to determine the presence of calcite within the rock samples they selected. I suggested that we integrate digital photography (we were still in the era of the old Mavica camera), online and field-guide research, and PowerPoint slide formats to create a "Virtual Rock Museum." Together we developed a vision for this project.

The students' Scholastic Reading Inventory indicated that 30 percent of this particular class read below grade level, so it was essential that we create more than one way of accessing and sharing information. Visual information would be especially valuable to this group. Two students in the class were classified as gifted learners. One student required special consideration for visual tracking problems. As in most classrooms, there was a wide range of learning styles, strengths, and challenges to accommodate.

Field guides on a variety of reading levels, from *National Audubon Society: Field Guide to Rocks and Minerals* (Chesterman and Lowe 1979) to Herbert Zim's *Rocks and Minerals* (1957), were offered along with highly visual books, such as *Rocks and Fossils: A Visual Guide* (Coenraads 2005). The classroom science text also offered an excellent auxiliary set of "science readers" (small, softbound books on a particular topic) on the subject of rocks and minerals. It seemed that coteaching and learning stations would be in order. As we explained the expectations to our students, we found that we were also developing a rubric that would help both teachers and students to evaluate the outcomes.

I inherited a collection of rocks and minerals from a friend some time ago and had added to it over the years, but had enjoyed the collection for its aesthetic, more than its geologic, value. I really knew very little about rocks. One of our school volunteers minored in geology during her college years and contributed a few special samples. (She was also extremely helpful in the preidentification stage of the rock study—a reminder to us all to make maximum use of the resources at hand. I didn't have to be a genius to realize that my impact as a teacher would be sizably diminished should a student ask excitedly, "Is it *metamorphic*?" and I could respond only with a dumb look.) With that in mind, I also read a few books on the subject and asked the teacher for a copy of the science text so that I could determine where the students were going with this particular study.

We housed the samples in a glass display case in the media center. Strategically placed at child height, just as students entered or left the media center, the display quickly gained the attention of our learning community. One student belonged to the Mineral of the Month Club (for more information, contact Mineral of the Month Club, 1770 Orville Avenue, Cambria, CA 93428; http://www.mineralofthemonthclub.org) and received two samples, with accompanying information about the specimens, each month in the mail. He shared some of his favorites. Other students brought in rocks from special trips: Cramer contributed a hunk of granite from a trip to Colorado; Jana (and I change names here to protect the less than innocent, as the passage will soon reveal) contributed a piece of obsidian, compliments of a trip to Hawaii with her grandparents; and other children added rocks gathered from the fields and pastures surrounding their homes.

While the classroom teacher gathered necessary materials for the hands-on experiments and demonstrated those processes to her students, I was busy showing the same students how to create a PowerPoint slide. The students particularly loved the wide selection of slide backgrounds and fonts. They already knew how to use the digital camera. Two cardboard trays, one lined with white fabric, and one with black, provided clear backgrounds for their shots. As we talked about what a good slide looked like and linked it with the teacher's expectations, we added to our developing rubric of excellence (see Figure 5.5).

I also wanted to target an appropriate Internet source for the fourth graders. A search led to the discovery of an online flowchart (http://www .lethsd.ab.ca/mmh/grade3c/Gr3Web/rocks_miner/indentify_rocks/iden-tify_rocks1.htm) suitable for our purposes. A series of questions—Does the rock have many crystals in it? Do you see sand grains or pebbles?—required students to closely observe their rock specimens. At one point in the flow chart, students were asked whether their sample fizzed when vinegar was added. Finally, the flowchart led them to a set of images to help them verify the identification of their samples. I devoted a class session to demonstrating the procedure and progress through the site.

After I spent a quiet afternoon taping and cataloging identifying num-

Name:_____Colleague_____

Here is what we said that an excellent slide should look like:

photo of rock	rock ID: classification: description:

Here is the rubric we developed:	2	1	Not yet
Name: I used two or more sources to identify my rock.			
Classification: I was about to use a source to classify my rock. I conferred with a colleague to classify my rock.			
Description: I included similes and metaphors and sparkling words.			
Technology: I took a clear and visible photograph of my rock. My slide includes a photo, text, and background. My slide is easy to read.			
Conventions: I used conventions correctly: spelling, punctuation, and sentence structure.			

Figure 5.5 Rubric of excellence for a rock sample slide.

bers on the bottom of each rock sample, the students were ready to select a specimen for research and identification. A rush ensued, as some pupils had cast a discerning eye on a particular sample and had mentally selected a favorite some time earlier. (In the chaos, Jana, unbeknownst to me, quickly and quietly selected the very rock she had earlier contributed, resulting in a brilliant, conclusive, and remarkably time-efficient identification of her sample. I did not catch this until much later.)

Our learning stations were in place: the laboratory, the text research center, the computer stations, and the photography station. The twenty-four students in the class rotated through the centers, snapping photos, accessing the field guides (some of the students needed guidance to select

Figure 5.6 Collaboration is natural for these research rock hounds as they work to identify and describe rock samples.

and use the most appropriate field guide for their personal use), and using the online rock identification flowchart (see Figure 5.6).

Our whole-group "experimentation station" reorganized into smaller groups to provide a one-to-one computer-learner ratio over the next several afternoons as the students configured their findings into slide format. While all the slides ultimately met the guidelines for the project—a visual image; sample identification; and the size, weight, and classification data requested by the classroom teacher—some were more detailed than others. For example, Haley discovered that her sample of marble was mined only from a specific spot in Greece, so she included that information in her slide.

With the slides linked together and a pithy copyright-free version of Simon and Garfunkel's "I Am a Rock" in the background, the virtual rock museum was born. The resulting project was shared at our school science fair. But that was not all. When creative minds converge, learning and expression can take many unexpected turns.

CRAFTING WORD PICTURES THAT SHINE

The samples generated so much interest among the students that we decided to "rock on" with a writing exercise that would help our fourth graders further prepare for their spring statewide writing assessment. Each student observed a rock sample and created a list of six to eight descriptive words. (Placing their rocks in paper bags, labeled with the students' names, added an air of oh-so-exciting secrecy necessary for the concluding exercise of this experience.) Using their favorite writing tool, the thesaurus, students "powered up" some of the adjectives that they had previously selected and developed a deeper awareness of multiple word meanings. For example, Maddie selected a quartz crystal for her writing project. She became confused when she went to her thesaurus to find a synonym for the word *clear* and found a list of verbs such as *remove* and *eliminate*. We went to the online visual thesaurus (http://www.visualthesaurus.com), which offers a sidebar of sample word phrases that viewers may select to narrow their choices. Maddie selected *the clear water* and a visual of descriptive synonyms such as *crystalline* and *transparent* appeared. The visual thesaurus became an important second source for students who had difficulty differentiating between word choices (see Can You See It? Thesaurus Skills for more information).

CAN YOU SEE IT? THESAURUS SKILLS

I don't just want my students to communicate. I want them to be able to communicate articulately and richly. That's empowerment!

We all know how elementary students love the descriptive words cute, nice, good, thingy, and stuff. One of my favorite tactics for banishing this two-dimensional vocabulary is an early introduction of the thesaurus. Believe it or not, my students love this resource. It opens up a world of words and meaning to them. Once they know how to use it and how it fits into their learning landscape, they come back to it again and again.

I like to begin with a standard student thesaurus in book format. As students access this, they reinforce basic skills, such as alphabetical order, guide words, and parts of grammar. They also pick up incidental information as they thumb through the pages and find that particular words catch their interest. (Sometimes I will ask them, "What did you find? And what else did you find?" In this world of direct and instantaneous information, we need to keep aware that potentially useful information is all around us.)

Visual and conceptual learners may have a more difficult time with the standard thesaurus than their auditory-linguistic counterparts. But they can be just as word savvy as the next child! The visual thesaurus projects an engrossing galaxy of words onto the computer screen; that galaxy shifts and realigns as students home in on specific synonyms. A navigation bar helps to narrow the focus and provides child-friendly context.

There are a couple of things to be aware of in conjunction with thesaurus skills. As students begin to access the thesaurus, their word choices may be, shall we say, a bit dramatic. To wit, Angel's interpretation of work as a restoration builder: "I spend boundless, murky days in my formidable job, repairing skanky houses. Sometimes I feel perspiring and dog tiring, but it's worth it!" This tendency will even out in time, as students become more sophisticated and selective users of this valuable writing tool. We can help them explore the world of words and respect their pace as they work through the process of finding and making new vocabulary their own.

The visual thesaurus is so compelling that I usually choose to introduce it after students are well versed in traditional, textual thesaurus skills. Students are so drawn in to that powerful visual of word-connectedness that they can remain lost for hours in the beautiful configurations and reconfigurations of word possibilities and lose sight of the writing project at hand!

The next step in the process was to learn about and incorporate similes. Our statewide writing assessment evaluates students on four points—focus, organization, support, and conventions. Vocabulary and writing tools that enable students to make comparisons, such as similes and metaphors, are rated at the higher end of the assessment scale. In addition, similes and metaphors are commonly used in junior fiction. Just as we teach our students to interpret and create visual images, the interplay of text and image in today's communication suggests that we must provide opportunities for students to interpret and create "word pictures" as well.

Further encouragement from the classroom teacher resulted in the addition of more detailed descriptions. Using a target as an image for her young writers, the teacher posted a bright, interesting photograph of an Amazon tree frog in the center of the target. Explaining to the students that each additional detail provided a more accurate description, she encouraged them to "shoot for the bull's eye" by adding powerful adjectives that created a clearer word picture. Students then used the same strategy to strengthen rock similes. For instance, one student's sentence, "My rock glistens like a star," became "My rock glistens like a faraway, twinkling star." (One of the phrases that I found especially creative compared a piece of smoky quartz to a "chunk of frozen root beer." Now, there's a powerful word picture.)

Each student incorporated his or her descriptive words and similes into four or five sentences and copied them onto an index card. Linked in paragraph form, these highly descriptive paragraphs were shuffled and redistributed to the students. Meanwhile, I had taken the rocks out of their bags and displayed them on the tabletop. Students had a great time reading the descriptive paragraphs and trying to match them to the correct rock sample.

What did our students learn through this guided research experience? They certainly met the scientific requirements of the study, learning how to create and gather data through a combination of hands-on experiments and reference materials. They increased their knowledge of rocks and minerals. They put their digital photography skills to use, and they integrated visual and textual information through a new technical skill—that of creating a digital slide. There was something here for everyone: the auditory learner, the visual learner, and the kinesthetic learner. There was a place to shine for the writers, the analyzers, the organizers, and the artists in the group. Clearly, this was a task-oriented project, with very specific requirements. Did it meet the standards for authentic research? Let's take a look.

Authentic research asks students to identify a problem to be solved, to locate, access, and evaluate information. It requires that they organize and synthesize their findings in a way that makes their work original. Students need to be able to present and share their findings with knowledge and confidence. Finally, they should be able to evaluate the effectiveness of their work. These students were asked to identify a rock sample. Working within a prepared environment, many of their information sources had been pre-selected. However, students selected from a range of rock and mineral field guides according to their reading levels and learning preferences. They had to use the information that they gathered in order to determine which, if any, experiments were necessary for further identification of the samples. The use of a PowerPoint slide format allowed students to present their findings both visually and in print form. Some students added additional details and information to their slide. They all enjoyed the artistic freedom to select fonts, backgrounds, and colors. Though the slides were linked together as a classroom project, each student presented his or her slide to the rest of the class, answering questions and fielding comments from classmates. Finally, students measured their final products against the rubric of excellence mutually established by the students and teachers to evaluate how well they met the goals of the research project.

INTEGRATED LEARNING, INTEGRATED LITERACIES

As teachers, we have always taken our role as the "source of information" seriously, but we have to remember that we are learners, too. If we determine what our students need to know, then we can look for creative ways to fuse those concepts and skills. By sharing a spirit of adventure with our students, we can willingly learn alongside them. In my role as an elementary media specialist, I have discovered that the more fully I integrate literature, visual literacy, technology, research, and problem-based learning, the more engaged students become. They want to show what they know.

Motivated by their ability to create and show, students of all ages can acquire, apply, and integrate information and skills, set standards for their own work, communicate in a variety of formats, and collaborate and coach one another. As they do so, they shift from the traditional role of passive recipient of knowledge to the twenty-first-century role of creative information seeker and communicator. Ordinary students become extraordinary learners.

Sound good? It is! After all, this is the way we learn and solve problems in real life—not through isolated tasks, but by effectively combining different sources of information to deepen our understanding and find solutions. As teachers, we use many resources and skills, along with a range of processes and tools, to develop units of study for our pupils. We collaborate, experiment, revise, and evaluate. We look for ways to reach the auditory learner, the kinesthetic learner, and the visual learner. Attending to their diverse needs becomes second nature to us, so we may not always fully analyze our means and methods. That's because we are applying real learning to a real job for a real purpose. And that's the ultimate goal of teaching—to lead our students toward a similar level of mastery.

Once you begin to cross-reference standards, integrate subject disciplines and literacies, and engage your students in their own learning, you will be amazed at how much you can accomplish within the demanding time frame of the traditional school schedule. All of the little preps for "bytes of learning" are traded in for creating the framework for educational experiences that are deep, purposeful, and meaningful.

Epilogue

Remember the Roman god Janus? The god of doors and gateways, he had two faces—one looking forward and the other facing backwards. He symbolized transition and progression, the shifting of one vision to another. He was also the guardian of growing children. His image comes to mind as I try to summarize the challenges and possibilities of the modern era in education.

Certainly almost every teacher cultivates, usually by necessity, eyes in the back of her head—that edu-radar that alerts us to imperceptible shifts in the climate of our classrooms and schools. We are continually building the foundation of learning, linking past experience with expanding expectations and broader responsibilities. But education isn't just changing; it's transforming in direct response to the accessibility of global communication. We can feel that transformation as it occurs. We are the ones who find ourselves standing in a doorway, gazing behind us with sentiment, comfort, and conviction. We fix our eyes ahead and feel what? Exhilarated? Uncertain? Fearful?

In this particular place and time, we have a special opportunity before us. Today's teachers must glean the best from the past—the best instructional practices, the bravest ideas, and, of course, the core disciplines—and usher them through the gateway to the future. What we teach may not change very much from year to year, but how we teach must be ever adaptive.

YOU CAN DO THIS, TOO

There is no magic formula for finding your way toward better teaching for today's generation. Though we live in an era of "suppress and assess," the very act of teaching is, by nature, creative and fluid. There are some key points that have been effective in my journey. At the center of the teaching experience is the belief that we work in a very human business and must approach education from a place of understanding—knowing students well, understanding what they care about, and appreciating the ways they perceive and interact with the world. When we recognize the visual connections they can and want to make, we will be able to help them access, organize, manage, and communicate information and ideas. We have to let go in order to grow.

A good starting point to learn more about the impact of visual literacy on today's learners and cultivate an awareness of its persuasive presence is the Partnership for 21st Century Skills (http://www.21stcenturyskills.org). Daniel Pink's book *A Whole New Mind* provides an excellent compass. It helped me see beyond my classroom and the present to better understand the long-term benefits of choosing to teach through a multimodal lens. The Center for Media Literacy (http://www.medialit.org) is another excellent resource.

These resources suggest some "über trends" in education—new ways of thinking about and applying learning and skills. We live in an information-rich society. That makes education more collaborative and more personalized. And *that* allows education to be more widely and evenly distributed. After all, children can tap into a wealth of learning resources at the touch of a keyboard or tap of a pad. The educational process is becoming richer and more creative—there are many platforms for expressing ideas, more than one way to solve problems, and any number of media-rich tools to bring ideas to life.

Medical research seems to support the value of these trends. We now know that intelligence is not fixed. We can continue to develop, and even to revitalize, neural connections through engagement in new and demanding learning tasks. Our brains actually strengthen in response to learning initiatives that challenge us to perceive, apply, or communicate information in a wide range of literacies and formats (Merzenich 2005). Diversity, creativity, rigor, and problem solving are the keys to engaged learning.

As teachers, we have always taken our role as the source of information seriously, but we have to remember that we are learners, too. Today's shifting educational landscape, fueled by creative, collaborative technology applications, requires a spirit of adventure—a willingness to let go and, often, to learn alongside our students.

That is what language arts teacher Cynthia Hildebrand discovered in her classes at Creekside Middle School in Port Orange, Florida, when one of my former students, Charlie Burgess, presented the class projects that he had developed with Adobe software. Hildebrand explained,

> Most kids come into middle school knowing how to put together a slide-show, but Charlie was producing on an entirely different level. We do a lot of project-based literature studies. When my students present their work in class, I always provide options on how they can share information and ideas—visually, musically, theatrically, or whatever medium they choose. I think it's important to give them room to express their ideas in their own way.

Eighth-grader Charlie responded to this invitation by creating media with Photoshop Elements, Illustrator, and InDesign software. "I took the guidelines for the assignment and stretched them 500 percent by applying technology," he said. "When you can create media that pops, you just blow your teachers away! Once you start creating this way, going back to traditional presentations seems subpar. I use traditional writing, of course, but I'm balancing it with visual information. I used to find stock photos and images, but I'm even doing my own vectoring now."

Charlie's knowledge inspired Hildebrand "to learn how to do it too." Teacher and student switched roles as Charlie began to coach her. Before long, the language arts teacher decided to incorporate InDesign into classroom publication projects and asked Charlie to design and lead a workshop for other students.

He was ready for the challenge:

> I figured, if I can teach a teacher, why can't I teach twenty kids just like me? I began by asking myself what I would want to know if I was just starting out. I tried to concentrate on the basics and show the other kids how they could build on those skills and continue to use them. I just told them, "There are a thousand buttons here, and you are going to be able to figure out how to use

900 of them." I used Captivate [software] to come up with a killer program—a tutorial that kids could move through at their own pace. They opened up the program and started working through it right away. Kids get so used to looking at an assignment on an overhead projector, step by step, telling students what to do, waiting for everybody to catch up. They are always being told how to do it, instead of learning how for themselves.

Charlie lives in an isolated part of our county and, throughout most of his childhood, has had limited access to technology at home. Samsula Elementary School opened a window to a wider world. He said,

I started back around second or third grade, working on class projects with Adobe Photoshop Elements in the school media center to build my own images—book covers, composite photos—things that really got the point across. I learned the foundation skills from teachers and students who had been around for a while. Then I just kept building on what I knew in order to tackle new software and processes. I like to learn through projects, putting it together, seeing if all the pieces fit, and figuring it out by trial and error.

Hildebrand said she had booked Charlie for other workshops. She continued,

What I see here is about a lot more than learning software. What I learn from students like Charlie, when I see what they know—well, it just amazes me. I see that everything today is so fast, and so visual. That's their world. And I think that students are missing out in the classroom, because it's just not being done there. I look at working this way, and I feel like I see where we need to go.

AS WE SAW IT

Writing this book has been a bittersweet experience. In the process, my teaching position was cut from full to half time as one result of budget cuts. Three-quarters of the way through the manuscript, further budget crises led to the school district's sudden decision to close the doors of our little school at the end of the spring term. The faculty and student body, the books and equipment, have been dispersed to various locations around the community. So it has been especially poignant to reflect on how far I have come through my experiences in that little media center, to tell the stories of real students, learning together, and to keep a bit of our world alive in these pages.

I asked some of my former students if learning through visual literacy continues to influence the way they learn and communicate. Haley, who was completing the eighth grade as I wrote this, told me she felt prepared to integrate visual literacy and technology into her schoolwork.

"I can make choices," she said. "I learned how to use lots of [software] programs, and I still mix them around, depending on what I want to say and how I want to say it.

"We use persuasive writing all the time in language arts class, and I like to create images that go with my writing. I just think it's easier for me to make visual presentations [in order to share information]. It makes me think more about what I'm learning when I connect the words and the pictures. It's more interesting, faster, and more fun."

Ana is now in seventh grade. She has kept up with her photography at home "mostly for fun." She reported that she does less computer work at school and more at home. "I basically think that a photo can create a story." Ana described how she used Photoshop Elements to develop an image, and then placed the manipulated images in PowerPoint, keeping a discerning eye for matching fonts and background colors with the intent of her images. "They most definitely give mood."

Ana acknowledged that she still has all of the digital imagery she created when she was in elementary school. "I look at those projects, and I can still remember what I did and what I learned."

A few weeks before the school closed, a tall young man walked into the media center. A rising senior in an international baccalaureate high school program, Abdullah was among the first group of students to explore visual literacy connections in our elementary media classes. While visiting, he looked around the media center and said without prompting, "This is my foundation. Everything I do now, and everything I plan to learn, stems from this place. I'm still building on what I learned right here."

And that is why we do what we do every day. That's why we show up, prepare, acquire new ideas and skills, and put our very best efforts into making our teaching as relevant and real as possible for this "eye genera- tion." When we engage their minds, capture their interest, and unleash their creativity, we empower them to make thoughtful choices, to com- municate richly, and to share ideas with confidence and purpose.

132

References and Resources

PROFESSIONAL RESOURCES

American Association of School Librarians and the Association for Educational Communications and Technology. 1998. *Information Power: Building Partnerships for Learning.* Chicago and London: American Association of School Librarians and the Association for Educational Communication and Technology.

American Library Association. 1998. *Information Literacy Standards for Student Learning.* Chicago and London: American Association of School Librarians and the Association for Educational Communication and Technology.

Association for Educational Communication and Technology (AECT). International Student Media Festival. http://www.ismf.net/ns.

Blank, Marion. 1983. *Teaching Learning in the Preschool: A Dialogue Approach.* Brookline, MA: Brookline Books.

———. 2006. *The Reading Remedy: Six Essential Skills That Will Turn Your Child into a Reader.* San Francisco: Jossey-Bass.

Burns, Mary. 2006. "A Thousand Words: Promoting Teachers' Visual Literacy Skills." *Multimedia & Internet @ Schools,* Jan/Feb. http://www.mmischools.com/Search/Default.aspx?Query=Thousand%20Words.

The Center for Media Literacy. http://www.medialit.org/.

Copyright Management Center at Purdue University. http://www.copy right.iupui.edu/quickguide.htm.

Daly, James. 2004. "Life on the Screen: Visual Literacy in Education." *Edutopia*, September. http://www.edutopia.org/life-screen.

Debes, John. 1969. "The Loom of Visual Literacy—An Overview." *Audio-visual Instructor*, October.

Dickeson, Linda. 2006. *CLICKstep Teacher Training Series: Photoshop Elements*. Bloomington, IL: FTC Publishing.

Digital Media Alliance Florida. http://www.dmaflorida.org/digital_media_is.html.

Eisenberg, Michael, and Robert Berkowitz. The Big 6. http://www.big6 .com/kids/.

Ellerbee, Linda. "Raising Media Savvy Kids." National Speakers Bureau, Inc. http://www.nationalspeakers.com/speakers/speaker_print .php?id=222.

enGauge. 2003. 21st Century Skills in the Digital Age (commissioned for NCREL by the Metiri Group). http://www.grrec.ky.gov/SLC_grant/ engauge21st_Century_Skills.pdf.

Entner, Roger. 2008. "The Increasingly Important Impact of Wireless Broadband Technology and Services on the U.S. Economy." CTIA International Association for Wireless Communications. http://files .ctia.org/pdf/Final_OvumEconomicImpact_Report_5_21_08.pdf.

Ganea, Patricia A., Megan Bloom Pickard, and Judy S. DeLoache. 2008. "Transfer Between Picture Books and the Real World by Very Young Children." *Journal of Cognition and Development*, September. Also available online at http://www.faculty.virginia.edu/deloache/Trans-fer%20between%20picture%20books%20and%20the%20real%20 world.pdf.

Horn, Martha, and Mary Ellen Giacobbe. 2007. *Talking, Drawing, and Writing.* Portland ME: Stenhouse.

Identifying Rocks. [Online flowchart.] http://www.lethsd.ab.ca/mmh/ grade3c/Gr3Web/rocks_miner/indentify_rocks/identify_rocks1.htm.

International Society for Technology in Education. 2008. National Educational Technology Standards (NETS). http://www.iste.org/AM/ Template.cfm?Section=NETS.

Jimerson, Lorna. 2006. *The Hobbit Effect: Why Small Schools Work.* Arlington, VA: School and Community Trust.

Johnson, C. Denise. 2003. "The Role of Child Development and Social Interaction in the Selection of Children's Literature to Promote Literacy Acquisition." *Early Childhood Research and Practice* 5(2). Also available online at http://ecrp.uiuc.edu/v5n2/johnson.html.

Lee's Summit, Missouri R–7 School District. Graphic Organizers. http:// its.leesummit.k12.mo.us/graphic_organizers.htm.

Leschak, Peter. 1991. Literary review of *Letters from the LeeLanau* by Kathleen Stocking. *New York Times,* January 27.

Merzenich, Michael. 2005. "Change Minds for the Better." *New England Journal of Medicine* 348(25).

Metiri Group/Cisco. 2008. *Multimodal Learning Through Media: What the Research Says.* http://www.cisco.com/web/strategy/docs/education/ Multimodal-Learning-Through-Media.pdf.

Mineral of the Month Club, 1770 Orville Avenue, Cambria, CA 93428. http://www.mineralofthemonthclub.org.

National Forum on Information Literacy. American Library Association. http://www.infolit.org/.

Ogle, Donna M. 1986. "K–W–L, A Teaching Model That Develops Active Reading and Expository Text." *Reading Teacher,* February.

The Online Visual Thesaurus. http://www.visualthesaurus.com.

Partnership for 21st Century Skills. 2007. 21st Century Skills Standards. http://www.21stcenturyskills.org/documents/21st_century_skills_standards.pdf.

Porter, Bernajean. 2005. *Digitales: The Art of Telling Digital Stories.* Denver: Bernajean Porter Consulting. http://www.digitales.us/index.php.

Pink, Daniel. 2006. *A Whole New Mind: Why Right Brainers Will Rule the Future.* New York: Penguin.

Poynter Institute for Media Studies. 2007. EyeTrack07 Report. http://eyetrack.poynter.org/.

Puttnam, David. 2007. "In Class, I Have to Power Down." *The Guardian,* May 8. http://www.guardian.co.uk/education/2007/may/08/elearning.schools.

Riddle, Johanna. 2004. "Sharing the Vision with Digital Photography." *Multimedia & Internet @ School*, May/June. http://www.infotoday.com/MMSchools/may04/riddle.shtml.

———. 2006. "Bookbinders: Fusing Technology, Image, and Literature." *Multimedia & Internet @ School*, March/April. http://www.mmischools.com/Articles/ReadArticle.aspx?ArticleID=11097.

Scholastic Reading Inventory. http://teacher.scholastic.com/products/sri/.

State of Florida Department of Education. 1998. Florida Sunshine State Standards. http://floridastandards.org/index.aspx.

"Technology Counts: STEM: The Push to Improve Science, Technology, Engineering, and Mathematics." *Education Week*, March, 27, 2008. http://www.edweek.org/ew/toc/2008/03/27/index.html.

Toffler, Alvin. 1980. *The Third Wave*. New York: William Morrow.

Weis, Jane Pullen. 2004. "Contemporary Literacy Skills: Global Initiatives." *Knowledge Quest* 32(4).

Wichita Vision Development Center. 2008. Children's Vision Information Network. "Learning to See—How Vision Develops." http://www.childrensvision.com/development.htm.

EARLY CHILDHOOD AND INTERMEDIATE REFERENCES

Aardema, Verna. 1983. *Bringing the Rain to Kapiti Plain*. New York: Dial Books for Young Readers.

Balliet, Blue. 2004. *Chasing Vermeer*. New York: Scholastic.

Bishop, Claire Hutchet. 1998. *Five Chinese Brothers*. New York: Penguin Putnam Books.

Bolan, Emily. 1992. *The House That Jack Built*. New York: Dutton.

Brett, Jan. 1998. *The First Dog*. San Diego: Harcourt Brace.

Carle, Eric. 1996. *The Grouchy Ladybug*. New York: HarperCollins.

Chesterman, Charles, and Kurt Lowe. 1979. *National Audubon Society Field Guide to Rocks and Minerals*. New York: Knopf.

Clarke, Ginger. 2000. *Baby Alligator*. New York: Grosset & Dunlap.

Coenraads, Robert. 2005. *Rocks and Fossils: A Visual Guide*. Buffalo, NY: Firefly Books.

Creech, Sharon. 2001. *A Fine, Fine School.* New York: Joanna Cotler Books.

138   Curtis, Christopher Paul. 1999. *Bud, Not Buddy.* New York: Scholastic.

Donnelly, Judy. 1998. *Tut's Mummy: Lost . . . and Found.* New York: Random House.

Dorling Kindersley. DK Eyewitness Books. New York: Dorling Kindersley.

DuPrau, Jeanne. 2003. *The City of Ember.* New York: Random House.

———. 2004. *The People of Sparks.* New York: Random House.

Fogelin, Adrian. 2000. *Crossing Jordan.* Atlanta: Peachtree.

———. 2001. *Anna Casey's Place in the World.* Atlanta: Peachtree.

Galdone, Paul. 1998. *The Three Little Pigs.* New York: Scholastic.

George, Jean Craighead. 1991. *My Side of the Mountain.* New York: Puffin Books.

Gulbis, Stephen. 2001. *I Know an Old Lady Who Swallowed a Fly.* New York: Scholastic.

Hatkoff, Isabella, Craig Hatkoff, and Paula Kahumba. 2006. *Owen & Mzee: The True Story of a Remarkable Friendship.* New York: Scholastic.

Hesse, Karen. 1996. *The Music of the Dolphins.* New York: Scholastic.

Hoban, Tana. 1971. *Look Again.* New York: Macmillan.

Kalman, Bobbie, and Jacqueline Langille. 1998. *What Are Food Chains and Food Webs?* New York: Crabtree.

Kipling, Rudyard. 1997. *Rikki-tikki-tavi.* Cambridge, UK: Candlewick.

Lassieur, Allison. 2006. *The Voyage of the Mayflower*. New York: Capstone.

Lauber, Patricia. 1995. *Who Eats What?* New York: HarperCollins.

Lear, Edward. 1996. *The Owl and the Pussycat*. New York: Putnam & Grosset.

Lowell, Susan. 1992. *The Three Little Javelinas*. New York: Scholastic.

Lowry, Lois. 1989. *Number the Stars*. New York: Dell.

Martin, Michael. 2005. *The Salem Witch Trials*. New York: Capstone.

Marzollo, Jean, and Walter Wick. 1992. *I Spy: A Book of Picture Riddles*, New York: Scholastic.

Mikaelson, Ben. 2001. *Touching Spirit Bear*. New York: HarperCollins.

National Geographic Kids: Online Adventures @ National Geographic. com. http://magma.nationalgeographic.com/ngexplorer/0203/ adventures/.

Olson, Kay Melchisedech. 2005. *The Assassination of Abraham Lincoln*. New York: Capstone.

Parish, Peggy. 1992. *Amelia Bedelia*. New York: HarperCollins.

Paterson, Katherine. 1977. *Bridge to Terabithia*. New York: Harper Collins.

Paulsen, Gary. 1987. *Hatchet*. New York: Puffin Books.

Riley, Peter. 1998. *Food Chains*. New York: Franklin Watts.

Rowling, J. K. 1997. *Harry Potter and the Sorcerer's Stone*. New York: Scholastic.

Rylant, Cynthia. 1987. *Henry and Mudge.* New York: Simon & Schuster.

Salley, Coleen. 2002. *Epossumondas.* San Diego: Harcourt.

Salten, Felix. 1926. *Bambi.* New York: Simon & Schuster.

Sendak, Maurice. 1977. *Seven Little Monsters.* New York: Harper & Row.

———. 1990. *Chicken Soup with Rice.* New York: HarperCollins.

Seuss, Dr. 1987. *The Cat and the Hat Comes Back.* New York: Random House.

Sharmat, Marjorie. 1991. *Nate the Great.* New York: Dell.

Shaw, Charles Green. 1998. *It Looked Like Split Milk.* New York: Harper-Collins.

Shehan, Sherry. 1996. *Barnacles Eat with Their Feet.* Brookfield, CT: Millbrook.

Spurr, Elizabeth. 1997. *The Long, Long Letter.* New York: Hyperion Books for Children.

Symes, R. F. 2004. *Rocks and Minerals.* New York: Dorling Kindersley.

Wallace, Karen. 2000. *Born to Be a Butterfly.* New York: Dorling Kindersley.

Wiesner, David. 1991. *Tuesday.* New York: Clarion Books.

———. "The Creative Process." http://www.houghtonmifflinbooks.com/authors/wiesner/process/process.shtml.

Wilder, Laura Ingalls. 2000. *Little House on the Prairie.* New York: HarperTrophy.

Zim, Herbert. 1957. *Rocks and Minerals.* New York: Golden.

SOURCES FOR STOCK PHOTOS

A word to the wise: the Internet is not rated G! Below are some sites that I
have safely accessed and used. I prefer to preselect a generous number of
photos and put in an accessible photo file on our school network drive.

FREE DIGITAL PHOTOS
http://www.freedigitalphotos.net

THE LIBRARY OF CONGRESS
http://www.loc.gov/library/libarch-digital.html

THE LIBRARY OF CONGRESS AMERICAN MEMORY PROJECT
http://www.memory.loc.gov/ammem/index.html

MORGUEFILE
http://www.morguefile.com

NASA
http://nix.nasa.gov/

THE NATIONAL ARCHIVES
http://www.archives.gov/research/arc/index.html

NOAA
http://www.photolib.noaa.gov

PD PHOTO
http://www.pdphoto.org

PICS4LEARNING
http://www.pics4learning.com

USEFUL WEBSITES

ADOBE PHOTOSHOP ELEMENTS
http://graphicssoft.about.com/od/digitalphotography/1/blps_prep.htm

ADOBE PREMIERE ELEMENTS
http://www.adobe.com/ap/products/premiereel/index.html

ARIZONA STATE UNIVERSITY LIBRARIES COPYRIGHT TUTORIAL
http://library.west.asu.edu/subjects/edu/copyrighttutorial.html

THE COPYRIGHT MANAGEMENT CENTER AT PURDUE UNIVERSITY
http://www.copyright.iupui.edu/quickguide.htm

DISCOVERY SCHOOL (KATHY SCHROCK)
http://school.discoveryeducation.com/schrockguide/eval.html

EASYBOOK AND EASYBOOK DELUXE
http://store.sunburst.com

FLORIDA SUNLINK INTERLIBRARY LOAN SERVICE
http://www.sunlink.ucf.edu

MAKING BOOKS (SUSAN KAPUSCINSKI GAYLORD)
http://www.makingbookswithchildren.blogspot.com

MICROSOFT POWERPOINT
http://www.microsoft.com/education/tutorials.mspx

PICASA
http://www.picasa.google.com

SCHOOLHOUSE VIDEO
http://www.schoolhousevideo.org/pages/storyboard.pdf

SOUNDZABOUND
http://www.soundzabound.com

STORYBOARD BLOG (KAREN J. LLOYD)
http://karenjlloyd.com/blog/2007/11/13/so-what-is-a-storyboard-anyway/

THE SUPER 3 (MICHAEL EISENBERG AND ROBERT BERKOWITZ)
http://www.big6.com/kids/K-2.htm